The

Great

Mind

Swindle

By

Tracey Pooley

Acknowledgments

Thank you to Graham for giving me the confidence to start my journey.

Thanks to Herman for being the biggest signpost of my life.

Thanks to Mark for prompting me.

Thank you to Jean Paul for sharing your genius.

Special thanks to Alison Wellman for the amazing illustrations

Thanks to Jess Macdonald for the editing.

Book cover by www.richsmallcalder.co.uk

Thank you to all my friends and family that have supported me and the wonderful people I have met along the way. The book would not have been completed without all of you!

With love Tracey

For more information visit
        www.TheHappinessClinic.co.uk

Contents

Part 4 NOW can you see your MIND SWINDLE?

Part 5 Things that might stop you changing

—

Introduction

Twinkle Twinkle Little Star, what you say is what you are…

"I am fat."
"I am stupid."
"I am unlikeable."
"I am worried."
"I am scared."
"I am depressed."
"I am anxious."

All of these I have uttered or at least thought about myself. These are what I like to call mind swindles.

The whole concept of the mind swindle is as complex as the workings of your mind and body, but I will explain each part as simply as I can and when you start to understand how your mind affects your body, it will become obvious. Your thoughts make you feel a certain way and with these feelings you are predetermined to behave a certain way. Without consciously thinking about it, you respond as you have done countless times before. If there is another way you don't see it. Even if you do, you don't know how to change things, and so nothing changes. You find yourself in the same old situations again and again. Life continues to go round in circles.

You are not designed to see your mind swindles. You probably are not even aware that they are there. The mind swindle hides itself. It is what is true to *you*. You are not designed to think about it. You do not question what you believe to be true. It just is.

Biologically speaking you are a mass of chemical reactions within a human shell.

The human body is like a machine with cogs turning, cells reproducing and a body remembering how to feel, what to think and what to do. We are continually responding to what is going on around us unconsciously, without being aware of all that is going on. We see life from our own perspective.

We tell ourselves what is happening and what we think about it. Without really questioning if it is right, we just do it. We do not question what we believe to be true. Why would we?

A simple example of this is a phobia. A phobic response is an irrational fear response to something that others might not be afraid of. Most people are scared of something: spiders, snakes, birds, heights, flying, and public speaking.

What are you afraid of? What provokes an over-the-top reaction in you?

You react like that because somewhere in your life you have learned to respond that way. It is unconscious and you can't help it. Others may see your behaviour as irrational but to you, that's the best response you know. You believe it is the right response. You have never considered responding another way. Maybe you have never considered behaving like others would in that situation. You unconsciously believe it to be the only response you have - but it isn't!

Your mind swindle tells you to behave that way. Unconsciously it works to keep you safe. It doesn't consider if it is *right* and it behaves as if correct, without question.

A phobia is a simple example but the mind swindle affects all of your life. It tells you what you think about everything that is going on around you and how you should behave because of it. You behave as you do because you have learned to do it that way before. You do it again because your mind swindle unconsciously tells you this is the best course of action, even if it isn't. You are programmed to repeat behaviour patterns. As you will discover, it is the way mind and body are made.

Even when you realise you're not right, you do not question yourself enough to change. You just continue. Again and again you find yourself in the same situations, doing the same things. You find yourself repeating past mistakes, almost

—

mechanically. You repeat behaviour because your mind swindle has told you this is the best thing to do, and you believe it without questioning if it is. It is only when you stop and look at the situation that you can decide if it is right. Most of us are unconscious as to why we do the things we do. We just act.

In order to change behaviours, we first have to make them conscious.

Most people can label themselves as something. *'I am under-confident', 'I am quiet'* or *'I suffer with stress'*.

Most people rarely stop to consider their behaviour and where it really comes from. They may have some ideas about why they are the way they are; where their personality has come from. You hear them say. *'I am like my Mum or Dad'* or *'I'm this way because…'* Each person has their story to tell about who they are and why they are the way they are. It is the story of their past.

It is their story that gives them their personality, the good bits and the bad. Personality traits, beliefs, thoughts, and the way we act - they all come from what we have learned to do in the past. What your mind swindle has taught you.

People rarely stop to consider how a thought can make them feel and how that feeling is translated into behaviour; but they are related.

Activity:
What are the thoughts and feelings that drive you?

How do they make you respond or act? It is your thoughts that make you behave unconsciously.

And as you behave, so other people will respond to you. They react as they know. They respond from their perspective of what they believe is happening. What are the thoughts, chemicals and beliefs that drive them?

Your thoughts are what make you the person you are. They are run by your beliefs and who *you* believe you are, the events going on around you and what you believe you should do in a given situation.

People behave as they know best. They know what is going on around them, or at least they think they do. They create thoughts about it, images in their heads. Thoughts create chemical responses within the body that make a person feel a certain way. These chemicals inhibit choice of behaviour.

In the Seventeenth century, Descartes did a deal with the Pope. Before then, medical people were not allowed to use dead bodies to practice on. They were not allowed to open up bodies to see how they worked as the body was sacred and belonged to God. Before the deal, man could only guess what was happening within the body, which is why such practices as bloodletting and using leeches were widely accepted as good medical practice.

This deal changed everything. Descartes could have dead bodies to dissect and study, on the condition that he left the mind (and spirituality) to the Church. From that moment, mind and body went in two separate directions. You see one type of doctor for the mind and one for your body. They do not really interact.

Obviously mind and body *do* interact. Your thoughts create a chemical reaction within your body. The chemicals make you feel a certain way and behave a certain way. Conversely, your behaviour makes you feel a certain way and think a certain way. They reinforce each other: proving your beliefs to be correct.

People do not stop to look at the thoughts and beliefs that drive them. They act the best way they know how but unconsciously. Not stopping to consider why they behave as they do. They just know they do. They speak in terms of 'I do this... I can't help it'. They think they have no choice.

This is a mind swindle!

There is always another choice. Becoming aware of the mind swindle will give you more choice to behave in a different way. Once you become aware of it, you have the power to behave any way you wish.

Are you sitting comfortably? Then let us begin…

FEAR

Firstly I would like you to introduce you to a concept you may not have thought much about before. You may have heard of it: False Evidence Acting Real. It is what we worry is going on or going to happen.

False

Evidence

Acting

Real

We can call it FEAR for short. FEAR is universal. We all feel it from time to time and for different reasons. FEAR is a basic instinct that comes from deep within our brain. It warns us of potential danger. For many of us, the FEAR response is triggered too much. This can manifest as anxiety or worry - adrenaline rushes or panic attacks.

To understand the concept of False Evidence Acting Real, let us go back to childhood. Lying in bed with the shadows from outside dancing on the wall. You hear a noise....

'Is there someone in here? Are they just outside? Will they try to get in?'

You feel sick. Your heart starts to thump. Your eyes search the shadows. You see something moving. You freeze! Your blood runs cold. Are they coming to get you... to murder you in your bed? Maybe they are robbers!

Your stomach feels like lead and your legs like jelly. You become paralyzed with fear as your heart pounds in your chest. Even if they don't see you, they will surely hear you. You hear the noise again. They are coming for you. You need to do something. Adrenaline spurring you on... What will you do? Hide under the covers, cry out or run from the room? You do it instantly and without thought before you are murdered.

The light is turned on. Light floods the room. The shadows disappear. There is no one there. A tree branch from outside scratches the window. You check under the bed and in the wardrobe. Nothing. You breathe a sigh of relief. *Phew!*

The evidence in this case was the movement of shadows. It triggered the mind. The mind searched for danger. It heard something, exacerbating your False Evidence Acting Real. You looked for other signs of danger. Your mind made more evidence. The FEAR was not real; it was just acting like it was real. This is a biological response to what you believe is happening. Just because we believe it is happening, it doesn't mean it is.

Sometimes we are mistaken. Sometimes, our beliefs are wrong.

Some of us fall into the habit of initiating our fear response too often. We suffer with anxiety. The trouble with fear is that it makes the body produce adrenaline, and adrenaline is addictive. Everyone has heard the term adrenaline junkie. Many people are addicted to adrenaline but because they are not jumping off cliffs or riding roller coasters they don't even realise it. We don't always get that high after it either. Our bodies just become used to feeling wound up and *adrenalised*.

Have you ever been afraid or worried? Have you ever been anxious or scared? It makes your heart start to thump.

Something happens... You think it. You see it. You hear it. You feel it. You FEAR it.

FEAR: That feeling in the pit of your stomach. That dread! Your thoughts race and your imagination conjures more thoughts into life. Ideas about what is happening.

Your heart has sped up - your thoughts too. What if *it* were to happen.... What would you do? You imagine scenarios. You get scared!

FEAR is such a dangerous thing. Your imagination sets off a chain of events. It sets your mind going in all directions. *What if this? What if that?* Your FEARS make pictures and your pictures make FEARS. They interact with one another, and still your imagination runs riot. Ideas - the pictures in your head become brighter. They look so real you respond to them as though they were real.

Your thoughts are the things that you listen to most of the day; your internal monologue. This probably goes on without you noticing it or what it says. And yet your thoughts run your entire system. They are the basis of your mind swindle - *your* thoughts, *your* chemicals, and *your* behaviour.

Adrenaline

What you think causes you to feel a certain way. What you think causes a chemical reaction within the body. It is those chemicals that drive your body and determine how you behave. For people who are worried or anxious, this is adrenaline.

Adrenaline is a hormone that is released when you believe you are in danger. We will look at this in greater depth later, but for now we'll just outline it and see if you recognise it. Adrenaline is part of the fight or flight response. Your body gets ready for action. When there is danger do you stand and fight or run away? Whatever you do, it is adrenaline that prepares you.

You first feel it in your stomach - that horrible feeling like lead. What you are actually feeling is your stomach shutting down. It is the adrenaline that makes this happen. When you are preparing for fight or flight, you do not need to digest food so your body prepares to expel it. You feel sick or need the toilet. You feel it in your chest. You heart starts to pound. Your breathing becomes rapid. Extra sugar increases your energy levels as you prepare to respond to the danger. Everything is racing as fight or flight kicks in. You can't think straight or focus. What do you do? Your hair stands on end. You sweat! All these symptoms and more are created by a hormone within your body: adrenaline.

When we are addicted to adrenaline our minds continually conjure thoughts, images and feelings by replaying past events or worrying about what is going to happen. They make you feel sick, and this is how anxiety starts.

How we use that adrenaline is how we have always used it. How we behave is unconscious. We do not think about it. We respond. It all starts in a split second and just keeps building. If you suffer with stress or anxiety, adrenaline has no cut-off switch. It will keep being produced until we use it up, and then comes a depressive low.

It is hard to think straight when your mind and body are racing. We do not consciously decide. We do whatever our mind swindle tell us. Our thoughts telling us what is going to happen. We make images in our heads that make our thoughts bigger and louder. They tell us how to behave. We think it is for the best. We respond instantly.

Are we always correct in how we respond? Could we be mistaken? Because we respond instantly, we do not use reason. We just act. The way we respond comes from our beliefs. What we know. Is our response always right? We believe it is but if you dare look at it... is it? Sometimes we are mistaken.

Do you dare look at it? Most people can find this scary. They don't want to look at it. Some develop coping mechanisms so they don't have to. It's a solution to their problem. But just like the shadows on the walls, not everything is as we think it is. Once you turn on the light you might see there's nothing there at all and it is just our imagination playing tricks on us.

At this point maybe we can stop and take a breath.

The Cooling Breath

For a simple exercise to help calm you when stressed or anxious, use The Cooling Breath. This is a yogic breathing exercise that maximises your inhalation and therefore the oxygen in your body. The whole exercise will distract you from your worries and cool the body down, slowing down the production of adrenaline. Once you know the breathing technique, you can use it anytime and anywhere by simply breathing a certain way.

To slow adrenaline down, simply breathe deeply in through your nose and blow it out through the mouth.

Breathing actually has three parts to it. You breathe in and you breathe out. After the outward breath there is a pause, which if you are stressed, is barely noticeable. Your body is waiting to inhale again.

Many people, especially when anxious, breathe small quick breaths from their chests, causing them to feel light headed or giddy. This is because they are breathing in and out so rapidly that the lungs don't have time to process the oxygen properly. The lack of oxygen inhibits rational thought and the adrenaline you are producing speeds everything up. It only takes a few moments of breathing fast and shallow from the top of your chest to start feeling light headed. How can you think straight like that?

The trick is to take deep belly breaths. The deeper you breathe, the more you will calm down. You may not have ever considered your breathing before. It is one of those unconscious things you do all the time.

Put one hand on your belly and as you inhale you are aiming to feel your belly rise first. If you are used to breathing high up in your chest, this is really hard at first and will take practise. You can then allow your breath to widen your rib cage and then into the chest. This maximises your breath and oxygen levels.

It may take a while to get used to breathing from the belly so stay calm and keep practicing. If breathing in three parts to the ribs and chest is too difficult just start with the belly, and the ribs and chest can come later. Don't give yourself more to stress over. Just breathe as deeply as you can.

Imagine the air going in through your nose, down your windpipe and filling your belly with air. Your hand on your stomach must rise first. Take time to practise belly breathing whenever you can. You may want to try it when you don't need it so you can get used to it.

Place your other hand in front of your mouth and making a circle with your lips blow hard against your hand. Tell yourself to relax.

Repeat and continue the exercise, slowly moving your hand further away from your face each time. See how far you can get it and still feel the cooling breath against your skin.

Now you are calmer you can think much more clearly. Try it. If you are used to breathing from the chest it may be tricky to start with. Practise it often. It will help whenever you feel anxious.

So you can see how easy it is to talk yourself into being scared, and how you usually behave at such times. By stopping and taking a breath you can look to see if there is anything to FEAR this time. By calming yourself you can decide what to do from here instead of doing the same old thing you always do.

Forget childhood - FEARS are scary to look at any age. However, if you stop long enough to look at your FEAR, you can look into the shadows. Is there anything there or is it your imagination playing tricks on you? This is essentially the mind swindle.

How can you deal with things better this time?

It is time to turn on the light...

PART ONE

The Mind Swindle

My theory

The human body is an amazing piece of engineering with masses of chemical reactions happening every second. Which chemicals are being made at any one time is largely dictated by a person's thoughts and belief system. These chemicals cause the body to behave a certain way.

Our behaviour is largely unconscious, led by our beliefs -without question!

Because of this, behaviour is automatic. There is no free will....

When you discover this, you have free will.

Let me explain....

The Basics

The basics represent my theory broken down into all of its parts. You don't need to understand it fully first time round as we go back over it all later in the book. Starting with the basics, we can then learn how to use them to our advantage to get what we want. You may find it helpful to jump back and forth between the pages to get a fuller and clearer picture.

The Biology

You may or may not know that the human body is designed around the individual's DNA. DNA is the code that tells the body how to grow. It determines everything from your hair colour and body type to whether you are prone to certain diseases. This code is divided up into sections called genes. It is thought that an individual has between approximately twenty to thirty thousand genes that are equally inherited from both parents.[1]

When fertilization occurs, so does a function known as mitosis, whereby a random 50% of both parents' genes are made into the very beginnings of a life. This embryonic life form will grow; cells divide under the instruction of the DNA and within 9 months develop into a beautiful baby. Much about this little life is already mapped out.

Life happens the way it happens and as it does, the course established by the DNA might be altered in some ways. For example, a person may have a "tall gene" within their DNA but if undernourished the body cannot grow to its full

---

[1] Davey Basiro, Halliday Tim and Hirst Mark: *Human Biology and Health: An Evolutionary Approach (2001)* The Open University

potential. So on a basic level, although DNA determines the body's growth and functioning, external influences can, and do, affect it.

It has been estimated that the body is made up of approximately 37 trillion cells, most carrying the person's DNA in its entirety within every cell's nucleus. Each cell has its own function mapped out by the DNA. There are nerve cells, blood cells, skin cells, organ cells, muscle cells and so on. Each cell is told by the DNA not only what type of cell it is but also, what its function is within the whole body.

The cell's surface is a semi-permeable membrane, which means very basic molecules such as water and nutrients are allowed to pass through it. For anything more complex like behaviour instructions, the cell has specific entry points called receptors.[2]

It was proved in the 1970s that on the surface of each individual cell are millions of receptors. These receptors are like micro-keyholes that allow information to pass through the cell's membrane and into the cell itself. The receptors are usually specific and only fit a certain micro-key. This is the information that goes into the cell. These are known as ligands.[3]

Ligands are made up of a string of amino acids,

[2] Simpkins J. I Williams *Advanced Human Biology*: (1993)
[3] Pert Candice PhD *Molecules of Emotion*: (1997)

some simple, some more complex, depending on their use. You might know them as hormones or proteins. All of them are pieces of information for the body. They are made in different areas and travel around the body, looking for receptors to connect with.

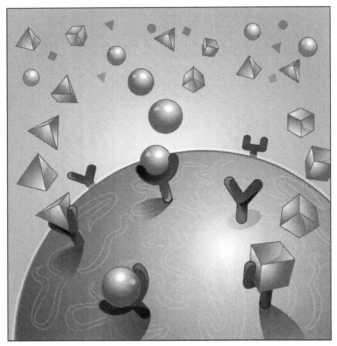

Figure 1. The receptor on the cell's surface will only fit a certain shape ligand.

When it finds its specific receptor, the ligand bumps up against it. The receptor is able to change shape slightly in some instances and they fit together like a key going into a lock. It is only then that the cell allows the instructions to enter.

This then sets off a chain-reaction that alters the cell. This minute change determines how a cell behaves and even how it divides, based purely on which receptors are occupied at any one time. If we apply this to the body as a whole, it affects how a person feels and behaves.

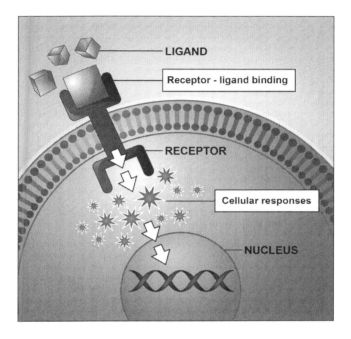

Figure 2. The ligand bumps up against the correct receptor and like a key fitting in a lock the information enters the cell

As an example, let us take adrenaline as an instruction for the body. Adrenaline is a chemical that is made when a person is aroused in some way either through excitement or danger.

Excitement creates a feeling of light-headedness, butterflies in your tummy and a racing heart. It also races when the body believes it is in danger. It creates a response called fight or flight whereby the body will either run from the danger or stand and fight. Whatever the body chooses to do, the instruction makes your body behave in the same way.

When the mind believes there may be danger, it unconsciously instructs the body to make adrenaline to help deal with the situation. A stimulus enters your brain through at least one of your senses. You hear, see, feel, smell or taste something that makes believe there is possibly trouble ahead. The stimulus comes into your brain to the thalamus, which is the central hub for all incoming stimuli. It then gets sent on to the relevant place within the brain to be processed fully.

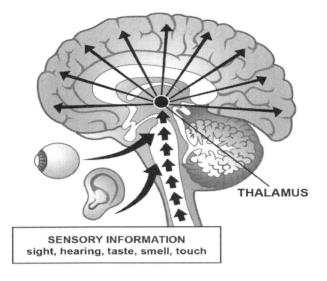

THALAMUS

SENSORY INFORMATION
sight, hearing, taste, smell, touch

Figure 3. Information enters the brain via the senses to the thalamus and gets sent on to other areas of the brain.

Whether you choose fight or flight, the body needs more energy so particular ligands travel to the liver and start the chain reaction that releases glucose (sugar) into the bloodstream. Other ligands constrict arteries making the heart pump faster. In other places ligands instruct blood vessels to open in order for more blood to flow. In order to face the emergency, they constrict blood vessels where blood isn't essential at that time and shut down any non-essential systems such as the digestive system.

If there is possible danger, the first part of the

brain's fear response sequence is alerted. This is called the amygdala (a_mig_dala). The amygdala are two small almond shaped parts of the brain -one on each side. Not only does the amygdala initiate the fear response but also controls where you store your memories. So if you hear a loud bang outside the house during the night, it reminds you to be fearful (as you have been before). It sends an alert by way of a chemical to the hypothalamus (hypo-thal-a-mus). The hypothalamus is just below the thalamus and is in charge of a multitude of tasks (sleep cycles, the balancing of the body, controlling blood pressure, body temperature and weight to name just a few). The hypothalamus in turn sends a chemical signal to the pituitary gland just below it outside the brain, which releases a hormone that tells the adrenal glands just above the kidneys to prepare the body for action.

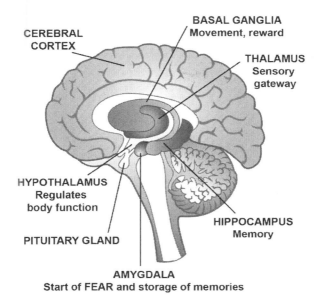

BASAL GANGLIA
Movement, reward

CEREBRAL CORTEX

THALAMUS
Sensory gateway

HYPOTHALAMUS
Regulates body function

PITUITARY GLAND

HIPPOCAMPUS
Memory

AMYGDALA
Start of FEAR and storage of memories

Figure 4. The different parts of the brain connected with the FEAR response

Along with adrenaline, cortisol is released which increases blood sugar, and is an anti-inflammatory to help the body repair after the emergency. The body gears up for action. Adrenaline and cortisol then flow through the bloodstream, attaching to different parts of the body such as the liver and the heart and make them act a certain way. They open up main arteries making the blood pump faster; our hearts race; we get a rush of energy from the extra sugar that the liver has stored; and in the eyes, our pupils dilate for better vision. This all happens unconsciously in a 50th of a second to prepare the body for fight or flight.[4]

So the moment you are alerted to potential danger, your body gets ready to deal with it. This is instantaneous and there is no conscious thought involved. This is called the low road to the fear path.

The higher road to the fear path is 10 times slower but still only takes a 5th of a second. Whilst the low road is in progress, the thalamus also sends the same stimulus to the hippocampus and prefrontal cortex to see if there is a memory of this situation being dangerous before. Have you had intruders before? If you remember a situation like this and it was dangerous, the hippocampus sends instruction to the amygdala that there is an emergency. If after looking for more information, you realise it was just *"that cat again"*, there is no emergency, the body slows back down. You return to a normal state. The high road in effect looks for more information to decide if there is any real danger.[5]

---

[4] Open University *Understanding depression and anxiety* (2016)

[5] Open University: *Understanding depression and anxiety (2016)*

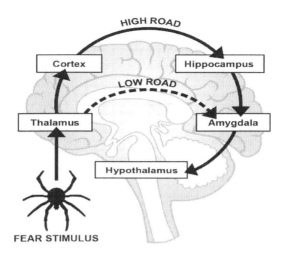

Figure 5. The fast and slow response to FEAR

When you are adrenalised your body is on high alert and you look for proof that danger is there. If you are used to looking for danger, you will be more likely to see it or worry that the danger is there. It becomes a cycle. You can stay on high alert and your stress response will keep firing. It is obvious really. People who suffer with anxiety worry about more things than people who are more relaxed.

Usually if it is discovered that there is no emergency, the adrenaline production stops and levels return to normal. There is a cut-off switch that prevents levels getting too high. This is called a positive feedback loop. The hippocampus tells the hypothalamus that no more adrenaline is needed. The cortisol is broken down in the blood stream and you return to your normal state.

If you keep becoming adrenalised, there is no cut-off switch. The positive feedback loop becomes negative. The cortisol, which is made alongside the adrenaline, damages the receptors in the hippocampus (which largely helps you to store memories) and prevents the positive feedback loop from working. The adrenaline and cortisol keep building. The extra cortisol not only damages the hippocampus receptors but also the cells themselves. This causes a person to suffer with brain fog.[6] This means the person suffers with poor mental clarity, forgetfulness and confusion.

Adrenaline continues to be made until you can't make any more. Your body then goes into adrenal failure and the person who is used to running on high levels of adrenaline finds they have no adrenaline to run on. This means less sugar, the heart stops racing, the blood stops pumping at the same rate. All this means the person stops moving at the same pace. They feel unable to move or think properly. They will feel depressed.

So how does the chain reaction start? With a thought, real or imagined: *'This could be*

---

[6] Open University *Understanding depression and anxiety (2016)*

dangerous or scary'; 'I am in trouble' or *'Oh, how exciting!'...* All of them elicit this kind of bodily response, the body's need for adrenaline.

This doesn't happen with just adrenaline. Each thought you have creates a need for different chemicals to be made, adrenaline being just one of them.

If your mind focuses itself on a particular thought or way of thinking most of the time, the body will be constantly flooded by a particular chemical, so too will the cells. The cell receptors on the surface can become desensitised, making them shrivel causing a loss of receptors. The body needs bigger hits of adrenaline to get the same response. This is how people's tolerance to chemicals including drugs can build.

Your body gets used to thinking worrying thoughts, which means you become more adrenalised. When your body is awash with adrenaline, behaviour is limited. It is hard to feel good if you are always thinking bad thoughts and it is always hard to think good thoughts if you are always feeling agitated. It's a cycle that continues to make you feel bad.

An excess of one chemical may leave you lacking in others. This will deprive you of different instructions on how to feel and how to behave. With the example of adrenaline, it makes the body shut down non-essential systems such as the digestive system. What will happen if your digestive system is continually shut down through too much adrenaline?

Serotonin is one of the chemicals that are associated with happiness. It affects how we feel, how we sleep, our appetite, and also muscle contraction and brain functions such as memory and learning. The chemical that makes serotonin is tryptophan and is ingested into the stomach by some of the foods that we eat. So when the digestive system is suppressed because of fear of danger, it stands to reason that so too is the making of serotonin. This can, if continued, lead to depression too.

This is just one example of how too much of one chemical alters the way a person feels and behaves. This whole process happens with every thought, good and bad, without the person consciously being aware of it. When the person gets into a certain way of thinking, they quite literally fall into a habit of feeling that way too.

Incidentally, it is my belief that this is how diseases like IBS occur. If the stomach stops and starts continually through stress and anxiety, it must surely be a cause for problems digesting food. A subject for another book maybe.

Activity:
Start to become aware of when a thought, be it real, imagined or a memory causes a chemical response in you.

Moods

On a more body-wide level, the different chemicals create a state of mind or mood. If you have adrenaline rushing round your body you will be agitated or anxious; if lots of serotonin is being made, you will be happy. Dopamine will make you expect good things.

Your mood fluctuates throughout the day so you can be rushed in the morning; frustrated by the late bus; bored at work; jealous of your partner; sleepy in the afternoon; excited by a dinner date and exhausted in the evening. All this in one day, with a myriad of other moods in between, depending on what concoction of chemicals are flowing through your bloodstream. The chemicals (or instructions for your cells) literally make you feel (and behave) a certain way.

Moods change quickly in response to external influences; that is to say people and the situations you may find yourself in. They are still dependent on how you perceive the world, yourself and those around you. So a pleasant situation will have your body making positive chemicals and put you in a positive mood, which makes you feel good. A bad situation will make negative instructions and put you in a negative mood

Your emotional state makes you think and act a certain way. If you feel frustrated you will think frustrated thoughts and act accordingly. If you are happy you look more on the bright side.

People have dominant moods (depending on what chemicals are being made by the body) in which they find themselves more frequently than others, how you most often feel. These dominant moods will either make you feel good or bad.

As well as this change in mental activity, all moods have a physiological manifestation. A happy mood will actually make you feel lighter, you will have a tendency to look up, you will frown less and smile more, your stomach will feel light and you will have more energy. A person who is in a negative mood will feel the opposite; not only heavy in the stomach but heavy hearted, they will look down more, their facial features may droop, their forehead will frown, they may find themselves with little or no energy to do anything. All these things are a physiological reaction to the way our mind is feeling.

The biology is that the thought creates a chemical reaction triggering different instructions to be made. They attach themselves to certain receptors of particular cells. This makes the cell act a certain way thereby making the body behave that certain way.
Our thoughts create these feelings or emotions. So thinking *'Oh I feel really fed up with this*

situation', 'I'm not sure that's a good idea', 'It really annoys me when they do that', will elicit one kind of bodily response. *'I'm looking forward to that', 'I am excited', 'I can do this, it is easy'*, will elicit others.

Activity:
Over the course of the next few days take note of your own personal moods. Give them each a name.

Are they positive or negative chemicals running your body?

How does each mood make you feel?

How does your body feel when you are in that mood?

How do you react to people?

How do people react to you?

Try keeping a diary so you can become fully aware of what your dominant moods are. Become aware of what triggers them.

What would you call the mood are you in right now?

Behaviour

Biology creates moods and both contribute to how we behave. It would be impossible for you to remain calm if you have too much adrenaline running through your body. In just the same way, it would be hard for you to act depressed if you actually felt happy. Biologically, the individual cell and therefore the body as a whole will have to act a certain way or at least within certain parameters.

If we feel frustrated we act frustrated, if we feel sad that's how we act. It is just logic really.

Humans are vastly complex pieces of engineering and for the most part what we are able to do is learned over time. Unless instinctive such as suckling; swallowing; breathing etc. A child is taught everything: how to eat properly; feed itself; dress; read and write; add and subtract. Everything is taught by repetition, thought and reinforcement. These are known as behaviour patterns.

Learning starts with someone with authority telling or showing you how. You can then try yourself but it is hard and a lot of thought must go into it. You then practise over and over with guidance until you can do it alone. The more you practise, the easier it becomes until you no longer have to think about what you are doing. It becomes unconscious.

Do you remember learning to tie your shoes and the level of concentration it took? You can now do it without any conscious effort on your part, leaving your mind free to think of other things.

Parents, siblings, peer groups and significant people in your life all have a part to play in your behaviour patterns. They are your people in authority. These people taught you what to learn and how to learn it. How they responded to your efforts will have impacted on how and what you learned. Positive reinforcement such as praise or positive behaviour towards your efforts will produce a different learning experience to one of disapproval or indifference.

Unless you have made a conscious choice to be opposite, you probably behave in some way similar to your parents or those who brought you up. For example, you probably share their political beliefs and respond similarly in certain situations. This is due to what they taught you as you were growing up.

Activity:
Take a moment to think about how were you taught to behave?

Triggers and pattern responses

When faced with certain situations our bodies learn to respond automatically without conscious thought. The brain stores everything -

all memories; feelings; actions and responses. When faced with similar situations, the brain learns to link the action with a response. This isn't a conscious thing. Neurons are fired, pathways made that when 'X' happens, I do 'Y'. It is part of your autonomic response system that means it is automatic. You respond instantly without conscious thought.

There have been many experiments to prove this is the case. The most famous was by Russian psychologist Ivan Pavlov, who conducted an experiment aiming to teach a dog to salivate upon command. Each time the dog ate; Pavlov rang a bell until the dog learned to associate the bell with food. Eventually the dog would hear the bell and salivate without any food being present. His brain expected food. This is known as a pattern response.

This is the same with humans. It is believed that 60 -70% of our behaviours are unconscious pattern responses[7]. A simple thing such as a piece of music can leave you feeling happy or sad. A red light automatically makes you stop and a green one makes you go. All without conscious thought, you are merely responding to what you have already learned before.

We could think of the trigger as a stimulus that causes us to feel or act a certain way. An

[7] Steven Heller *Monsters and magical sticks* (1987)

unconscious reminder of a way we have behaved before. It is something that triggers a memory; something that has made us feel or act a certain way before.

A song can make you feel happy or sad depending on what it unconsciously reminds you of, so too a raised voice makes you excited or afraid. A tone of voice, a look, a touch, a taste or a smell… all of these have the capability to trigger a biological response. Whether it is bad or good depends on the memory to which it is linked. The amygdala and the hippocampus remind you of how you felt last time, and you respond instantly without a second thought.

Your autonomic nervous system links things together, so that when X occurs it causes a Y response. You have no control over what it links together. It is, like the name suggests, automatic and takes place at an unconscious level depending on what is happening at the time. This is part of the reason your mind swindle is hard to unravel. You may respond to something a certain way and not understand why. Something in your past has made it happen that way and the more you respond to the trigger, the more entrenched it becomes as a pattern response. You fall into a habit of behaving a certain way in certain situations or with certain stimuli.

For the most part, these responses are learned

over time. If we become used to something happening a certain way, then we come to expect it, and respond instantly without any conscious thought to whether the reaction is for the best.

Sometimes a situation causes you to react so severely that it can take just this one-off incident to cause your body to respond that way over and over again.

Take a phobic response. A phobia is an irrational response to something learned usually from a one-off incident. People's brains and bodies react irrationally to something that others would know as harmless. Almost everyone is afraid of something however irrational it may be. The human brain is capable of learning instantly to be afraid.

When faced with a traumatic experience it remembers it, so that whenever faced with a similar situation it responds immediately, in the same way it has previously. It is a survival technique that the brain uses to keep you safe. If you were once upon a time terrified by a spider, the next time you saw one you will unconsciously remember and be afraid again.

Logically a person may know the given response isn't necessary; but illogically has learned to respond that way, they can't help themselves. You replay the fear instantaneously without conscious thought.

Any response to a situation then has the potential to become a trigger to behave a certain way. The more often a situation occurs that triggers the same response, so the connection between the two grows. How quickly the body learns to react is dependent upon the intensity of feelings the situation evokes. The stronger the feelings, the quicker it remembers. It is a survival technique.

Let us imagine that you once had an anxiety attack at the doctors. The next time you go, you start with the thought (conscious or unconscious) that you suffered the last time you were here. You worry it might happen again. You dread it. Your stomach turns to lead. Your heart races. You panic that it's going to happen again and guess what? You do not choose it to happen. It is an unconscious programme. This is how your mind swindle brings your thoughts to life. Your unconscious memory started it happening and now you have linked the two together, it is more likely to happen over and over. It will become a behaviour pattern. Your thoughts: "It always happens…" and so it does.

We could at this point deconstruct the response as a chemical reaction on a molecular level again, but it is enough to understand that the way we learn to deal with events in our lives is based on how we feel about the event. The chemicals that we create limit the way we are able to react. Our bodies become accustomed to behaving and feeling a certain way. The body is running unconscious programmes.

If this is the case, each event in our lives teaches us something about ourselves: how to act, how to feel or how to respond. A person can only act the best way they know how: the way they know how comes from experience. Until you have learned it, there is no other way to behave. Responses become automatic through repetition fuelled by chemicals – emotions for your body. And all this is driven by what you are thinking.

Because so many of our pattern responses are unconscious, we behave without thinking. We do not use our free will.

Activity:
Take a moment to bring the unconscious into the conscious.

What do you respond instantly and unconsciously to that you wish you didn't?

Beliefs

Beliefs are you. They are the things that you are sure of.

You are sure of so many things. What you think of the world and the people around you; who you think you are and what you think of yourself; what you believe is right or wrong; what makes you happy; what makes you afraid… Your belief system is everything you have learned to be true, even if it is not. Beliefs have many different origins. Parents, siblings and peer groups helped us learn what is right or wrong, or at least what they believe is right and wrong. But other people too, (the way they behaved towards us and the rest of the world) also shape our belief system and what we believe to be correct.

There are many different ways we learn. We are sat down and taught, guided by people and shown the way. We learn by repetition, by remembering information over and over again until it sinks in. How quickly we learn is dependent on the importance we place upon this information. Whether years long or a once-in-a-lifetime occurrence, everything has the chance to teach us something. From times tables to thoughts about yourself. They have all been learned over a period of time. Because we believe it, we see it as truth and so it is – from our perspective.

Whether they are or not, we feel that our beliefs are 100% correct. This is obvious. If this were not the case, we would be forever questioning them. At the time of believing them, our whole system is setup on a subconscious level to prove our beliefs correct. If we believe we can't do something we are more likely to quit quickly, believing there is no point in trying and therefore reinforcing the belief we can't. Our body responds to these beliefs as though they were a certainty. Whether we believe we are in danger or are in a particular mood of expectation, our body reacts the only way it knows how – chemically.

Beliefs are both created and reinforced by the world around us. We have grown up listening to different authority figures telling us that their way is the best way. We grow up believing that what they tell us is correct: it becomes true – even if it is not. Once we hold that belief, we react to it without a second thought. Like a piece of music that makes us happy, we respond unconsciously.

Our bodies are run automatically through our autonomic nervous system. We breathe, our heart beats, we grow and repair our bodies without ever being consciously aware that we are doing it.

We take in the world around us through our senses – what we see, hear, feel, taste and smell. This is run by our peripheral nervous system – again unconscious.

Every second, the human brain is bombarded with millions of pieces of information through our senses. All that our eyes see at any one moment; how our body is feeling; the different temperatures and pressures against our skin; what our ears can hear; tastes and what smells are around us represent the information that makes up our world as we know it. Of course it would be impossible to consciously log all the data, so the brain sets out to make sense of it. It does this within certain parameters that it believes are correct.

Our brain can't possibly cope with all that information so it ignores great swathes of it. In fact, NLP creators Richard Bandler and John Grinder suggested that the brain can only take notice of just seven pieces of information[8] – give or take a couple – at any one moment. For example until you choose to take notice of it, you are not aware of how your foot is feeling at this very second. Try it! How does it feel? Can you feel it resting against something or can you feel the air against it? Maybe it is covered in something. How does that feel? Whether you take notice of it or not, that feeling is still there, you just delete it from your conscious thought as unimportant. If there were a nail in it, then you would notice it. Now ignore your foot and take notice of your hand in the same way. Do you see how it works? The feeling in your foot fades away as you take notice of something else by the feeling is still there. Your brain just ignores it.

---

[8] Bandler and Grinder *Using your brain for a change:* (1985)

Your mind chooses to take notice of what it believes to be important at the time. Through repetition, it has learned what to remember. Anything that doesn't fit into our belief system is deleted as irrelevant. The mind wouldn't allow you to see things differently to how you believed they are. You would constantly have your beliefs called into question.

Activity:
What does your mind take notice of?

What is unconsciously important to you?

Are you beginning to see your mind swindle yet?

Differing Realities

In 1931, Alfred Korzybski first coined the phrase "The map is not the territory." Simply put, this means that although we think of something a certain way, it is just our reality. How we personally think of it. It is not the same for everyone. In reality the territory is different for everyone. A snap shot, one perspective – our own or how we see it.

Each person takes in and interprets the world individually and depending on past experience and what is important to them. We all walk our own path.

One person would describe Christmas in a completely different way to another. Someone who enjoys it would possibly think of the building excitement, the colours, the feast and tree. Someone who hates Christmas may think of the crowded shops, the expense and the thankless task ahead. This is because we all see it through our own set of values and judgements that come from our past experiences. Our map of Christmas is not how Christmas is for everyone, just us. So if I said, "Christmas is coming", then it would get a different reaction from different people. Same day of the year but seen differently. Everyone is correct from their point of view. We just have different realities of the same thing.

This is how we all interpret interaction the world around us. After seeing someone looking at them, a person with low self-esteem may see it with a level of concern. 'Why are they looking at me like that?' Someone with confidence will see the same look in a completely different way. 'That person wants to interact with me.' An angry person may wonder if they are looking for a fight. It is our belief system that causes the reaction.

All information comes through your senses - sight, hearing, touch, taste and smell. What your brain takes notice of is what it deems important. It works on a self-preservation basis, so if you react strongly to something, your brain will identify it as a priority to take notice of.

How you behave is dependent on what you believe and this is reinforced by triggers. It is the trigger that causes the biological response. Whether information for adrenaline or serotonin to be released or any other instruction, your thought makes the biology happen and you feel and act a certain way. This is all down to your own perspective, which is run by your belief system and what you have learned so far.

Activity:
The words we use to describe our realities are very important. These are the words that dictate how we think and what we know.

How do the words that you use to describe yourself, make you feel? Positive or negative?

These are the words that drive the chemicals that run your body. As we already know, with certain chemicals running our body we can only act a certain way. Choices seem limited.

Beliefs create behaviour

How you behave is linked to what you believe and what you think. There is often no thought involved, it is unconscious. You act out what you believe. If you believe you should hit first and ask questions later, you will. If you believe you are unlikeable, that's how you'll behave.

Your brain has learned over time what to think and how to behave. It is not even aware that there may be a different choice of action. This is part of your mind swindle. Imagine you are a nervous person. You might say, *'I hate talking to new people. I don't know why I just do. I can't help it.'* It is this mind swindle that makes you behave a certain way.

Occasionally the rug is pulled from under us. Our eyes are opened and we are forced to question our beliefs about ourselves or something else. On the whole however, we continue to be the person we believe we are and act without thought, or simply ignore what we are shown without acknowledging its truth.

This is how we run our lives, every second of every day. Our bodies do as they are told; the driving tools for this are our thoughts, unconsciously running everything. This is your mind swindle.

The first thing a thought does is to create an image in the mind's eye. Some images are more vivid than others. The more vivid the picture, the stronger reaction you will get. Whether the image is real or whether it is imagined makes no difference; the brain cannot tell the difference.

As an example, imagine something bad happening. When you look at the image, how does it make you feel? Now try it with something good.

Your brain makes an image and from there, it sends out messages to the rest of your body - information on how to act. In a split second your body starts to react to the image. If it has reacted to it a certain way before it will do so again, unconsciously and without a thought as to whether it is correct in doing so. It has become a pattern response.

These images are created by our thoughts and what we believe to be correct. It certainly feels real to us. This is because of all the chemicals being released around the body - instructions on how to respond. The body always acts as it knows from past situations. Simple things unconsciously become triggers for behaviour. What the mind responds to is what it knows. We have learned in the past how to behave in certain situations. The particular instructions being made will reinforce a certain way to behave.

All this reinforces behaviour patterns and in turn reinforces the belief that it is correct to act think and feel that way and so we continue to behave the way we do - a self-fulfilling prophecy. It all becomes a cycle, each reinforcing the other. This is how the mind swindle keeps itself hidden.

Activity:
What beliefs do you have?

How do they make you behave?

Or you can turn this on its head: Where does your behaviour come from?

What belief makes you behave like that?

Is it correct?

Every behaviour serves a purpose

Action may be thoughtless sometimes but it always has a purpose. At some point in the past, a person has learned that this is the best way to behave and so they do, unconsciously and without question.

Consider the bully either at home, in school, in the workplace or in the community. The bully knows that by behaving as they do, they will gain something. Demeaning behaviour will make the other person feel small and more importantly will make the bully feel bigger. Aggressive behaviour is designed to stop the other person fighting back. They have learned that if a person is scared, they are more likely to act subserviently.

The victim of the bully stays quiet because they dread what may happen if they say something. They have previously learned that staying quiet is easier than sticking up for themselves, and so they do; without thought of whether this is the right thing to do. This behaviour doesn't come from nowhere. That person has learned to behave like that in the past.

We see behaviour from our own perspective, but if we could zoom out and see other people's behaviour from their perspective we would see that it has a purpose. It doesn't excuse it; it just explains it. If you had walked that path and learned all the things they had, maybe you would be acting the exact same way.

This doesn't mean the choice of behaviour is the best choice there is. It is the best choice of action as far as that person is concerned at that time. Behaviour is largely unconscious -it comes from all we have learned so far. What we believe is the best way to behave, even if we haven't given it much thought.

This behaviour might have adverse effects on the person or others but because it once served a purpose, it is believed that it still will.

Unconscious triggers remind us of the best way to act and the behaviour continues until it is somehow consciously stopped. If you have never learned another way to behave, how would you know how?

Another person learns from their experiences how to behave but that only fits in with their belief systems, their upbringing and their

—

perspective. That too is only correct from their perspective and what they believe is correct. They have a different reality. We all behave the best way we have learned so far.

Activity:
What behaviours do you have, that you don't like?

What do you believe they are doing for you?

Are they working out that way?

What are they actually doing for you?

Thoughts create!

Every thought creates a chemical reaction within your body. It makes you feel a certain way. With those feelings, you behave a certain way – a way that fits with your beliefs – a way you have learned over time depending on your personality.

Activity:
Consider this thought …

"I think they do not like me."

How does it make you feel?

You create a response to that thought - a feeling. The chemicals run round your body. You make

---

pictures in your mind and remember things that have been said that prove that you are right. (Your mind swindle) Your feelings get stronger. Your thoughts continue...

"What shall I do?"

You create a behaviour. How do you act? Responding to triggers and pattern responses, you act as you know –how you have learned to. You do the best thing you know.

"I don't know what's going on."

Any action causes a reaction. How do they behave?

"What's going to happen next?"

You respond again. They react to your behaviour.

What is the outcome?

As you can see, thoughts **do** create!

This happens with all your thoughts. You think it – therefore it's true. Your thoughts determine how you feel and the way you behave. Because you live in a world with other people, they react to the way you behave.

I once worked with someone who believed their
mother preferred their sibling. They grew up
believing this and it affected all areas of their
life... It made them feel worthless and gave them
very low self-esteem. As an adult, every time
they phoned they would hear tales of how well
their wonderful sibling was doing. It made them
feel pretty useless. It made that person wonder:
'What is wrong with me?'

After working with them they saw there was
nothing wrong with them and the fault was with
their mother. They saw what a decent person
they were. They changed their belief.

Consequently, their thoughts changed. They felt
differently and acted differently towards their
mother. As a result their mother responded

differently to them. Their relationship improved so much that for the first time ever this person enjoyed visiting their mother.

On a visit, their mother confessed to being very unhappy. It turns out that the other sibling was making her very unhappy. She didn't prefer them at all. She was dominated by them and had nothing else in their life so consequently talked about the sibling all the time.

This person grew up believing one thing and lived her life by acting on this belief. All this time they were wrong and they never knew it.

Exercise:
Consider another thought…

"I think ……"
(Insert your own belief. You can pick anything you believe about yourself)

What does your thought create?

How does it make you feel?

How do you behave because of your thought?

You behave as you know.

How have you learned to behave?

How do others react to you?

Can you see how significant the wording is that you used in getting the response you did?

Is the response you got the one you wanted?

What was the outcome?

What does your behaviour do for you?

Does it do what you intended?

If you believed something different, you would think a different way, feel a different way and therefore act a different way. Because of this people would react differently to you. But that would be a different you, with a different past and having learned different lessons along the way. You act unconsciously to your thoughts that are created by your belief system. What you have learned so far. This is your mind swindle but your mind swindle may be wrong.

In everything you do, you are acting unconsciously. Your mind swindle drives everything and up until this point you were not even aware it was there.

Conclusion

So here we are; understanding the very fundamentals of our being and what it is that drives us.

In summary:
- Your belief system is the very essence of what drives you.

- Your beliefs create your thoughts and they in turn make you behave the way you do.

- It is your thoughts that create the chemicals that drive you.

- This chemical reaction causes the body to behave a certain way.

- With certain chemicals being made, it can only behave a certain way and it always behaves the best way it knows how.

- Your mind swindle stops you questioning if you are right.

- You are stuck with dominant moods, reacting unconsciously to triggers from the past

- You only remember your past from your own perspective. What you *believe* happened.

- Your perspective upholds your beliefs.

- The more you think and behave a certain way the more automatic it becomes to behave that way.

This is your Mind Swindle!

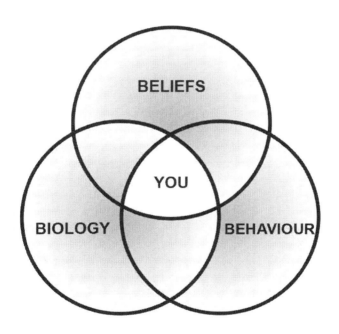

Biology creates moods; moods determine our behaviour. Behaviour is run by our belief systems. Belief systems run and determine our thoughts and it is these that determine what chemicals are made; how we feel and how we behave. It becomes a cycle.

Your body continues to do what it does day after day. You are stuck responding automatically to unconscious behaviour patterns. You do not consider if it is right to do so or if there is another choice of behaviour.

You lose your free choice about how to behave.

When you discover how the mind swindle works and that you are actually swindling yourself from behaving as you wish, you have free choice to behave anyway you like.

Food for thought before you move on...

Can you see how your mind swindle has stopped you from changing your behaviour?

How could you improve your life by changing a mood or behaviour pattern?

How would you like life to be different from how it is now?

Take some time to consider these questions.

Jot down some ideas if it will make things clearer to understand.

Part Two

Thinking of changing

You are at the point when you know that there are some things about your life, you would like to change. We get to these times when we realise that we want something to be different than it is now. Maybe you want to act differently, feel differently or live differently?

Some people are so busy being unhappy that they do not stop to consider what would make them happy. It is such a simple notion but because of your mind swindle it is often overlooked. To think about it fully you need to follow a few simple rules.

Reflections

When asked how life could be different from now, people often reply in the negative. "I don't want this" or "I don't like that."

This is a fundamental mistake because the human brain doesn't see the negative.

Experiment
Q. If I say **Do not think about the colour red**. What do you think of?

A. You have to think about the colour red in order to think about the command.

Saying **"I must not eat chocolate"** What do you think about?

"Cheer up, it might not happen" What do you imagine?

Your brain has nothing positive to work with. In order for your change to happen, you have to be consciously aware enough, to make things change. If you haven't thought about what you would like to change about yourself, how can you change it?

There is more to it than how you *don't* want things to be.

How *do* you want things?

If you don't give yourself an idea of how you *do* want things to be, how will you know what to change? It is so obvious and yet we are all guilty of making this mistake.

Exercise:
What do you want?

Take some time to think about it in positive terms. Jot down some ideas.

Giving Up

Every behaviour serves a purpose, that is to say it has positive intent. Fundamentally, we are programmed to gain something from what we do. Some people might say they want to lose or give something up: weight; smoking; a fear – all examples of losing something.

'I don't want to think about smoking anymore. I want to give it up.' Where is the positive intent? What are you thinking about? It is bound to fail!

The trouble with giving something up is the mind connects it with losing something – missing out on something. Why would it want to lose or give up anything? It would be far happier to gain something. If you believe you are losing or giving something up, where is the positive in doing so? Why would you work hard to lose something?

So the trick when thinking about giving up or losing something is to turn the negative into a positive. Think about the gains. So losing weight isn't about losing the weight but more about gaining confidence by looking and feeling better about yourself. Giving up smoking is about feeling healthier. These are just ideas. An individual knows what advantages there are for them.

Exercise:
What are your advantages for change?

What will you gain?

> Write down as many things as possible that you will gain from making the change.
>
> Think of all the *positives*.

Changing You

The other mistake is trying to change other people. Wishing another person would not (a negative!!) behave a certain way or wanting them to be different is the obvious thought. Someone else changing would mean you would not have to!

Everyone acts primarily for their own gain. We believe that our behaviour will do something for us (even if it doesn't turn out that way). It serves a purpose. Because we are interacting with others, they see our and their behaviour but from their own perspective, their reality, their belief system and what they have learned so far. It is their map of the territory. You are behaving that way (from their perspective) for a certain reason. This might be a completely different reason as to why you are behaving that way, but it is *their* perspective they are reacting too. They can't help but see it that way. They have a different reality to you.

Their behaviour best serves their purpose, or at least what they have learned best serves their purpose. They are reacting to their past and what they have learned is the best way to deal with a situation, whether we think it is or not.

People react to how they perceive our behaviour. How they react to us is a consequence of our behaviour. If you want others to change their behaviour towards you, then you may have to first change your behaviour towards them. Who else but you could ensure the correct sort of behaviour for *you*? Only *you* know what's right for you. Once you start to change, people will respond differently and consequently you will get your change from them. But *you* have to change first.

Exercise:
How could you change your behaviour in order to change someone else's?

Remember to think about it in positive terms. If you "Wouldn't do that anymore", what would you do instead?

Changing

So the first step is to know what you *do* want rather than what you don't want and to state it in positive terms. Some people know what they want straight away. Others need time to think.

Exercise:
If you know or think you know, take a moment to clarify what it is.

What is it that you want to change?

Say it out loud, maybe in front of a mirror. See how it feels.

Do it whenever you can. It only takes a second. The more you do it, the more the mind will connect to bringing about a more positive behaviour. You have to retrain your brain to think another way from the way it is used to.

If you do not know, then take a moment anyway and I will give you something to think about.

Emotions

The chemicals that are running round our bodies are responsible for how we feel. On a very basic level, each chemical is information for your body. It tells each individual cell how to act. While adrenaline causes your body to work harder, speed up, make sugar, get your body ready for action, it is just as possible to make other chemicals to run your body.

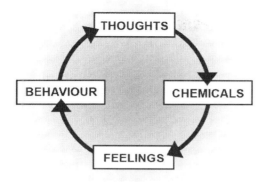

Exercise:
Your mood will affect the way that you feel.
What is your dominant mood or moods? On the
whole do they make you feel good or bad?

Remember at the moment, your body is used to
feeling this way. You habitually think a certain
way, which creates the same old chemicals.

Would you prefer a different mood? Too feel a
different way?

What emotion would you like more of? Do you
know how to get that?

With too many chemicals that make you feel
negative running round your body, it isn't
always easy to stop and decide what it is that
you want.

This is your chance to think about it.

The Cooling Breath

This was covered in the introduction but it is a key point. Most people are running on adrenaline. Their mind swindles cause them to worry or be anxious by creating fears in their head and believing them to be definite truths.

This is a simple exercise to relax you more. Do you remember the cooling breath? Have you practised it lately? This is a yogic breathing exercise that maximises your breath inhalation and therefore the oxygen in your body. This exercise distracts you from your worries and cools the body down, slowing down the production of adrenaline. (Remember for people running on adrenaline, there is no cut-off switch, it just keeps building.)

In order to slow adrenaline down, simply breathe deeply in through your nose and release through the mouth.

Many people, especially when anxious, breathe small quick breaths from their chest, causing a lack of oxygen to the body. A lack of oxygen inhibits rational thought and the adrenaline you are producing speeds everything up. It only takes a few breaths of breathing fast and shallow from the top of your chest to start feeling light headed. How can you think straight?

The trick is to take deep belly breathes. Put one

hand on your belly and as you inhale you are aiming to feel your belly rise first. You can then allow your breath to widen your rib cage and then move into the chest. This maximises your breath and oxygen levels. It may take a while to get used to breathing from the belly so keep practising. If breathing in three parts into the ribs and chest is too difficult, just start with the belly, and the ribs and chest can come later. Imagine the air going in through your nose, down your windpipe and filling your stomach with air. Your hand on your stomach must rise first.

Place your other hand in front of your mouth and making a circle with your lips gently blow against your hand. Tell yourself to 'Relax'.

Repeat and continue the exercise, slowly moving your hand further away from your face each time. See how far you can move your hand away and still feel the cooling breath against your skin.

Now you are calmer you can think much more clearly. Try it. If you are used to breathing from the chest it may be tricky to start with. Practise it often. It will help whenever you feel anxious.

Just like Pavlov's dog, telling yourself to relax will become a pattern response and so with practise, just telling yourself to relax will become a conditioning. Your mind will link the word with the feeling and you will be able to do it on command; but that of course takes practise!

You don't need the hand in front of the face but it is a great way to focus your mind on the task. You can use this anywhere, whenever you are anxious, *anywhere*! Take a deep breath in and blow out through the mouth. Tell yourself to relax. Let the adrenaline slow and regain rational thought.

Moods

Remember your state of mind is your mood, how you are feeling – tired, bored, frustrated, excited and a myriad of other moods – all changing throughout the day. Moods might also be described as personality traits - you can feel like you are in a confident or uncertain mood after all.

Exercise:
What state or mood would you like to be in more of the time?

Remember moods have a physical manifestation. Do you know how that mood feels? If not, can you imagine? It is you that wants this after all.

How would you behave with others?

How would your head feel? Your stomach? Your eyes? And your heart?

What would you look like?

How would you stand, walk and hold yourself?

How would you appear to others?

How would you talk?

Remember if you have not done this before, your mind and body won't know how. It is up to you to teach them. You are training yourself to change. If you are unsure, you can imagine. Your body may not be used to making those chemicals that make you feel a certain way. The more you do it; the more those instructions for the body will be made, and the easier it will be to get into that mood. It is practise that will make it perfect.

You can start practising whenever you get the chance. Alone in front of a mirror or with other people. Change the way your body feels. Your body learns by repetition so the more you do it, the easier it is to stay in that mood. How would you feel in certain situations? How would you behave? When people start to respond differently, how would that make you feel?

Sometimes something may trigger you into an older, unproductive mood that you don't want to be in. When you notice you are back in the old mood, you can work hard at getting yourself out of it. If you have adrenaline, use the cooling breath to cool your body down again. Change back to how you stand, walk and talk in your new mood. Take your breath and change - it is the only way to change.

If it doesn't work, take a look at why. What is stopping you? Is there a problem that you need to resolve here? A belief that is stopping you? This is your mind swindle playing tricks on you.

People can become disheartened and give up but if you do that, nothing will change. Learn from your mistakes and keep improving. It will become as natural as your old behaviour. Remember moods are learned so what has been learned one way can be relearned another. It just takes practise, but you have to try hard for it to work.

Behaviour

Why do we act the way we do? There is a reason behind everything we do. We believe it will do something for us even if it doesn't pan out that way.

Our history has taught us to behave a certain way - maybe even unconsciously. If we act a certain way to a given situation, we will remember it. The more we act this way; the more we remember it and the more this behaviour becomes automatic. We don't think about how to act in certain situations, we just act and behave unconsciously.

The flip side to this is that it is only learned behaviour. If we had a different history, we would believe different things and act a different way, think a different way. Those realities could be poles apart.

We are able then to ask ourselves what we would like to change. How could we behave differently? You become consciously aware that when 'X' happens you do 'Y' and the outcome is 'Z'. If you don't want 'Z' then you have to change your response to 'X'. When we start to change our behaviour, it will change our moods. We will start to believe things can change and so they will. The answer then is to become more aware of how you behave now and how you want to behave.

Exercise:
What behaviours do you want to change?

How do you want to behave?

What stops you? This is your mind swindle. The bit we need to fix

---

Beliefs

There is a school of thought that is beautifully illustrated by Steve Heller PhD in *Monsters and Magical Sticks – There is no such thing as hypnosis"* that everything is hypnosis.[9]

He made the point that hypnosis is just an altered state of consciousness. Where you have come to believe something as true, even if it isn't. Imagine the stage hypnotist: *"When I touch your right shoulder you will believe you are a chicken."* The more the hypnotist touches the subject's shoulder, the more it becomes natural to behave that way.

Imagine now the working hypnotist: *"When you think of smoking you will smell the burning tar and feel sick"* The connection is made and cigarettes smell disgusting and make you feel sick.

Now think of driving down the road with a driving instructor for the first time: *"When you see the red light you will stop"* The connection is made and after practise, the action becomes unconscious. If you drive a car – you do not think about taking your foot off the accelerator and applying the brake, you do it automatically.

Now think of the adult and child: *"You can't do anything right! Why can't you just behave for once?"* What is the difference? If they are told this repeatedly – hypnosis or not – the connection is made and the child learns a truth. They are *useless*. They *can't* behave and so they don't! Are they stupid and useless or have they just been

---

[9] Steven Heller *Monsters and Magical Sticks:* (1987)

hypnotised into believing that they are?

Exercise:
Where do your beliefs come from?

Your beliefs come from what you have been told or what you have learned in the past. You were in effect hypnotised into believing certain things were the truth. If you found something hard, what did you learn? What if you found something easy? Beliefs are reinforced or shattered by what happens in the world around you.

What did the people around you do to help those beliefs become your reality?

This is where your mind swindle comes from. What you believe is the right way to think and behave. Just because you were taught these things were true, doesn't mean they are. You were taught by people who were taught by other people. None of it is necessarily true, but you behave according to your beliefs.

Everyone has a past and *that* is where we learn our belief system. Situations or events where we learned something significant in our lives created certain behaviour patterns. Right from birth we learn every behaviour pattern: how to walk, talk, and feed ourselves.

This is also true of our personal beliefs. What

you believe about yourself and the world in which you live; was formed by what parents or other significant people in your life thought. You have unknowingly taken on their beliefs and made them your own without ever consciously thinking about it. The people with authority in your life have taught you this is correct. This is the way it is, and unconsciously you react to it without a second thought.

Activity:
Think back to your childhood and these significant people. Can you remember how they treated you and how that felt? What did they teach you about right and wrong? What did they teach you about themselves and yourself? Their behaviour still affects you in some way now.

Did you have any siblings? How did they act towards you? How did you interact with each other?

What about childhood friends? How did they act? What were they like to be around? Did you feel you had to behave a certain way in order to fit in? Were you the strong one that everyone else followed? Were you too quiet to have many friends? Where did your behaviour come from?

What about teachers and the community where you lived. What was their expectation of you? How did their expectations affect your behaviour? Where and when did you learn to

---

behave like this?

As you were growing up, what did you learn about yourself and others? How important are you? What is the right way to behave? What do you think of yourself? Without necessarily being consciously aware of it, all these answers come from childhood teachings. How you behaved once and behaved that way again and again until yourself or others label you as being that type of person.

Just because they come from childhood teachings doesn't mean they are correct. It is just that time in our lives that we are learning the most. What we learn comes from the situations we find ourselves in, and what we remember. This is how we behave; the best way we know how. Once we start looking at our behaviour we become consciously aware of it. Then we can decide if it is still best for us or if there is a better way.

Exercise:
What did your childhood teach you?

What were you hypnotised into believing?

Why were you taught that? What did the other person gain?

Was that the right thing for a child to learn?

If the answer is yes, are you sure? Or have you been hypnotised into believing that?

Is it part of your mind swindle? Why you behave as you do.

Differing Realities

How we react has become an automatic response. We react to the world as we have learned over time. The same tone of voice could be linked with danger or fun depending on what you believe it to mean. A look from someone may trigger a physical response unconsciously remembered from your past.

You react to the world as you see it. How many times has someone said to you, *"I didn't mean it like that"*? This is when someone says something to you and you take it to mean something else. As we have already seen, each of us has differing realities. How we view a situation is dependent solely on what we believe or think is happening. Our world: Our perspective. What we believe a situation to mean. But sometimes we are wrong. Sometimes we misunderstand. Sometimes there is another way and it is only our mind swindle that stops us seeing it.

How we see a situation isn't necessarily how other people see it. They are seeing it from their own perspective, which comes from their own history and beliefs about the world and what is happening.

It is only past experiences that make us see it from this perspective. It is our past that dictates how we behave – our choice of action. Unconsciously we behave as we believe we should; without a thought as to whether it is right. *'Of course it is'*, we say! There is no thought process involved. Remember up to 70% of our thought processes are unconscious pattern responses. We rarely stop to consider the truth.

Believing is seeing

We always believe what we see. It *has* to be true if it is in front of us, right? The thoughts we have are reinforced by the images that flash in our mind's eye. Our body reacts to what we see as though it is a certainty. But is it? It is simply one perspective. Would someone else see it a different way?

Without your history and all that you have learned, how might you act? Think? Feel?

The answer is that without your history reminding you how to behave in a given situation, you are free to act a different way. The choice is yours.

Seeing is believing!

The Experiment

That being said, if we believed something else, would it change the way we felt?

Here is an experiment you could try now. Take a moment and just think of something you would like to change, something positive. Even if you do not believe it is possible now you can still use your imagination.

What is it you want?

Can you make an image of it? Our thoughts are accompanied by images that are made up in certain ways – these are known as sub-modalities, named by Bandler and Grinder in the 1970's[10].

Sub-modalities

Images in your mind's eye could be:

Black-and-white or colour,
Moving or still,
Framed or surrounding you.
You may see the picture through your eyes or observe as a bystander. You may even be in the picture.

---

[10] John Grinder *Transformations:* (1981)

The picture can be fuzzy or clear,
Big or small,
Zoomed in or panned out,
In a central position or over to one side.

These sub-modalities can be altered and will affect how you react to the image. Try it with an image of what you want.

Change the colour and see how it changes the feel of the picture.

Swap a moving picture to a still and see how it alters things.

Play around with all the sub-modalities and see how it changes the way your body reacts to the image.

Put a frame around it or take it away.

If you are in the picture, take yourself out so you are just watching it or put yourself into the picture.

Zoom the picture in or pan it out; make it big or small.

Change the position of the picture so is over to one side or in the middle.

Spend some time playing around and make it as lifelike as you can.

Are there any sounds to that image?

How does the image make you feel?

Not everyone is this visual so some of you may prefer to tell yourself what you want. Imagine sounds and smells to help make the picture more vivid.

Give the image as much detail as possible.

When do you want this?
Where?

How will it affect you?

What would it be like?

How would you feel?

Perhaps now you have a better image? Try playing with the sub-modalities again (See above).

Does what you want appear more attainable now? How we represent something in our mind affects how believable it is.

Conclusion:

- The brain does not see the negative. State what you want in positive terms.

- A person doesn't want to give up or lose anything. What are the gains of change?

- You cannot change other people, just yourself.

- How do you want to respond differently to others?

- You have been hypnotised into believing your beliefs are correct but are they? Would another you with another history, believe something else?

- Who taught you what to believe and therefore how to behave? What did they gain from it?

- Every behaviour has positive intention. What do you *believe* you gain from your behaviour? Are you correct?

- Thoughts create chemicals – chemicals create feelings – feelings create behaviour – behaviour creates thoughts…. It is a cycle.

- Your dominant moods keep you behaving this way. You can change them by changing your thoughts.

- Seeing is believing! Become aware of any images that play in your mind and any sounds that go along with these images.

- The images that run through our heads play a very important role in how we are feeling and for the most part, we are not even aware that they are there; let alone unconsciously driven by them!

- Whether real or imagined, an image flashes into your mind. This creates a chain reaction causing your body to start responding to it.

- Unless it is told, the human brain can't tell the difference between what is real and what is imagined. The chemical reaction is the same.

Food for thought before you move on:

It's time to decide now. What do you want? Take some time to think about it in positive terms. Jot down a few ideas maybe...

Imagine the type of person you'll be...
Imagine how it would feel...
How you would respond to situations?
How does it feel?

If you worry about how you will change, this is your mind swindle playing tricks on you. You will learn how to let go of those fears as we go through the book.

PART THREE

TIME FOR A CHANGE

Most people get to a point in their life when they realise what they want. And even if they dare not admit it, they also know how to get it. They know how they will have to act. They know how they will have to make a change.

But this is as far as they get. They do not stop to consider changing their programming. They are not even aware that they can! This is how life is. I am *this* person and *this* is my life. This is because they have been hypnotised into believing that *this* is their life. Significant people in their life have taught them this and now they do not stop to consider another way. Because of their mind swindles, people remain stuck. The only way for change to take place is to adjust how your mind and body have been programmed. To alter the way you behave in different situations. Once you learn that you can, you are one step away from doing so. As you rid yourself of previously learned behaviour patterns you can learn new ones. Simply by deciding that you are going to change; enables you to make that change. Until you make that decision to change, nothing will.

Responsibility

So you are now at the point you can see where you have come from. How you have got here may not have been your fault, but you are here all the same. You can see how you are responding. You have identified yourself as *'I am X'*. You know that you want something different from that which you have now; you know what you want to be: *'I want to be Y'*. Who is going to get it for you? Is there a fairy ready to wave a magic wand? Do you think the person or persons responsible for you being where you are now, are going to sort everything out? Maybe it suits that person that you behave the way you do. Everyone works for their own gain or what they *believe* is their own gain.

If you want things to be different for you; then you have to take the responsibility for changing things for yourself. Start to reprogram yourself to behave differently in a certain situation. You are ultimately responsible for your own actions and your own happiness. You must do what is right for you. It is time to free yourself of your mind swindles.

If someone else is causing your problems and you want them to behave differently from how they do now, you are asking them to be different from who they are. You are asking them to change their programming. If you want them to change solely for you, then you are asking them to be someone they are not. This will ultimately lead to unhappiness on both sides. *They* have to want to change in order to change, the same as you.

They may not know that their behaviour is wrong. They are seeing the situation from their past and their reality. They may have been brought up to believe that their behaviour is correct – normal even. If they have never been taught that it is wrong to behave *that* way then how would they know?

In order for them to change their behaviour they have to know what you want, why you want it, and why it is important to you. Being able to sit down and discuss it is very important. People approach difficulties from their own perspective but in order for them to change, they have to see things from another perspective and, of course, so do you.

Communication is the key. Emotions can run high and when they do, it is difficult to see other perspectives to your own. Use the cooling breath to calm yourselves and listen to why change would help and what is hard to change and why. There is always a reason.

It is up to that person to decide whether any changes fit with the type of person they are. You personally cannot change someone else's behaviour. It is part of their programming and their past. They are responding the best way they know how. You can point out behaviour and how it affects you, but it is up to the individual alone to change it.

And it is up to you to decide if you can accept their choice.

Is it time?

Maybe you have reached the point you want things to change. You have had enough of being like *this*, feeling like *this*, acting like *this*. You want something else. There is no time like the present to start to change, but it has to start with you.

In the past you have not been aware that things could change, but things are different now. If now is the right time for you to change, then you can do!

Exercise:
Remind yourself what it is you want. Make sure it is positive intent "I want…" If you have a negative intent "I don't want…" Change it to a positive.

Voice it to yourself alone, with friends or maybe in front of a mirror. Become aware that since you have decided to make some changes, things can start to change.

What do you want? How do you want to change? Once you start thinking about changing; the neurons in the brain will start to fire and make connections, building chemicals that will give you other choices of behaviour.

Voicing your change will make it more real. Your brain will rewire itself and you will start to have new choices. It is up to you what you choose from here but without changing something, nothing will happen.

What's stopping you?

People say it cannot be that simple otherwise I would have changed by now. This is not true. You were never aware of what you know now. What is stopping you? YOU ARE! Your mind swindle! Your history, your beliefs, your thoughts, your chemicals, your behaviour patterns. Once *you* start to change, things will start to change.

Behaviour Patterns/Pattern responses

Just like triggers, pattern responses make us behave a certain way. When 'X' happens I/they do 'Y'. Pattern responses are what we have learned in the past. So a bully will know if they shout they will get their own way, and an under-confident person will have learned not to stick up for themselves to avoid conflict. They may not even think or imagine the consequences, a mere look or a tone may trigger the feeling of dread and that may be enough to prevent them going any further.

This behaviour comes from the past where that feeling of dread was followed by something bad happening or being told something bad might, or will happen. Everything is linked by whatever the trigger is. The unconscious reminder of how it has been before. Since it happened that way in the past, the brain links them together believing it will always be the case. It will happen that way again. It becomes a pattern response.

This is called the Past/Future Loop.

Exercise:
Have you started to notice behaviour patterns or pattern responses?

Are they helpful to you?

Do you want to change your response?

PAST/FUTURE LOOP

Do you sometimes feel that nothing changes? Because of your behaviour patterns, your life goes round in circles and you end up behaving the same way over and over again.

People have a tendency to forget that **now** exists.

—

It is the moment we are living in. It is today. It is this moment, doing whatever it is we're doing. But where are our heads in the here and now? Most people live in the past or the future.

We take the situation we are in now and relate it to something that happened in the past. Because the situations are similar, we expect the outcome to be similar. You would not expect something different to happen. We foresee the future. We tell ourselves what is going to happen. Imagining it! Your body cannot help but respond the same way again. What you have done before, you will do again. Without thinking you respond now the way you always have. You would not change the way you behaved unless you chose to do something different. You are responding to old triggers.

You look at the situation with a set of beliefs about what is happening. You have been taught over time what happens in situations like this. From the moment you think *'I think this is going to happen'*; you start responding. You do not stop to question whether you are correct. What is happening just fits into your belief system. It makes you feel a certain way. Your body starts making chemicals. You have merely acted that way before and so do it again bringing about a similar outcome as before. The result – nothing changes. It is your mind swindle tricking you again.

People foresee the future as they expect it to happen so it fits with what they believe -their mind swindle. Logically they would not anticipate what they do not believe; it would not occur to them to try to do so. They know what to expect by what they have learned in the past.

The future has not happened and this in itself can cause anxiety. People like to know what is going to happen and so consequently like to guess and second-guess the future, listening to their thoughts and discussing it with others, building scenarios that play out in their imagination. There is something comforting in knowing what will happen next. They do not wait to see if it happens. Their behaviour automatically fits in with their belief system and the future they foresee.

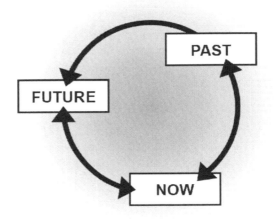

Figure 7. The past future loop

Because it is unconscious, people do not even consider whether their response is correct or try to rationalise it. It just responds -chemically, physiologically, behaviourally. How it has learned to behave over time.

Imagine you want things to be different. You want to act differently to how you do now. If you are used to things being one way, thinking of changing may cause anxiety. Maybe you worry how those around you will receive this new behaviour.

Thoughts creep in as to what might happen; that IT could happen. Remember the brain doesn't know the difference between what is real and what is imagined. You imagine what *may* happen if you change. Your mind sees it as real and your body reacts to it as though it is real, and to you it is! This alone is enough to stop you acting the way that you want, and so you go round in a loop.

Maybe you have tried changing before but nothing really *did* change. Maybe things got better for a time and gradually got worse again. We now know that you were responding to old triggers again. But if you think you know the outcome before you start, why would you try and change it? ... And so the cycle continues.

Remember any FEAR will make adrenaline. Adrenaline is used for fight or flight. Your body prepares for action. Your body acts as it knows, whether this is fight or flight, it only has two choices.

From where does this imagined future come? Perhaps the outcome has played out before in the past and you expect it will again. Maybe you have been told it will happen or brought up to believe it happens this way. You look for the signs. The mind takes notice of what it considers to be important.

How does all this affect your behaviour?

The past/future loop happens all the time without you ever really being aware of it. It is part of your mind swindle. It's within every one of your pattern responses.

Life has a tendency to go round in circles.

You find yourself in the same situation, acting the same way again and again. This is your mind associating with either past or future events - pattern responses.

These cycles will either make you feel generally good or generally bad depending on your life circumstances. The only way to change the cycle is to change something: a thought; an image; a belief or behaviour. Changing one thing will alter the cycle and give you the chance for things to be a different way.

—

Where do we go once we have broken the cycle? Our behaviour can either spiral up altering things for the good, or spiral down for the bad.

If we remain aware that we have started to change things and congratulate ourselves on any small change, we build positive reinforcement that we did not have before. We can build on the small changes and make bigger changes, allowing ourselves (and our moods) to spiral positively upwards.

By not staying aware of these changes, you will not see the changes. If you cannot see a change, nothing does – behaviour continues. Changes in how you act, (however small) will alter things but you need to start looking for, and recognising any change.

Exercise:
Can you remember a time when you have used a past future loop?

A time when you behaved a certain way because you were sure what the outcome would be – because of how things happened in the past.

Triggers

Remember, you have learned over time how to act. Anything from a tone of voice to the sight of something, to a taste or a smell, can trigger an emotion in us. It reminds us of how it was in the past. The memory triggers a feeling in us. This chemical change makes us respond a certain way.

We can start to become aware of triggers and the way they make our body feel. They are all around us once you start noticing. Once you start to become aware of them, you can choose how to react. Look at the belief that makes us respond in that way. Is it real or False Evidence Acting Real? Before you react a certain way, decide if it is how you want to react. It may have been the best way of behaving in the past but is that the best way for you now? If you can stop yourself from responding unconsciously, you can choose to respond differently.

If you usually react one way to the trigger, what would happen if you did the opposite? What stops you is your automatic pattern responses, but if you are aware of them you can start to change them. You can stop yourself and choose to behave a different way.

Exercise:
Take some time now to look at the triggers that you respond to. How do you respond unconsciously to stimulus that you wish you didn't? E.g. When 'X' does 'Y', automatically I do 'Z'...

An Exercise in Eliminating Past Triggers

Triggers always cause you to act a certain way. It is both an automatic and unconscious response. Something triggers that response. You are reminded to act that way by something or somebody else. It is what you have learned.

The answer is to eliminate the trigger.

Rather than respond as you always have, stop. Look at it. Change the response.

Exercise:
What trigger would you like to change?

How would you like to respond?

What started that trigger? Can you remember?

Who or what taught you to respond that way?

For what purpose?

What did they gain?

What did you believe that you gained?

Is this still true?
Is this a helpful trigger?

What causes you to respond as you do?
What is the belief? Is the belief true or were you

mistaken at the time when it formed?

If you heard the story about what happened (rather than it happening to you) what would you say about the situation? The belief that was made; is it correct if it belonged to someone else?

What is the driving emotion? How does the stimulus make you feel? Can you give it a name?

If you could point to the feeling within your body, where do you feel it? Is it in your stomach, your heart, your head or your hand? It could be coming from anywhere.

Now at this point people get uncomfortable. They don't like the feelings this evokes and the body produces adrenaline. Things start to race. They would rather not feel like this so their mind starts to talk, distracting the person from focusing on the feeling. It is at this point most people look away and continue to use the trigger. They believe it is too difficult to deal with, but they're wrong. They just need to work through it. It doesn't take long if they stay focused.

You need to stop the mind talking and just watch the emotion. It may have a reason as to why it makes you feel like it does but it doesn't need any commentary at this point. Stop distracting yourself with thoughts. When you are focused on the internal dialogue, you can't focus on the feeling properly.

Stop and look at the feeling it creates. It doesn't need to be analysed as right or wrong. It is merely an old behaviour pattern. You just have to watch the emotion. See how it changes. Ride the emotion and allow it to run its course, keeping yourself fully focused on the feeling.

The emotion is like a wave rising before it falls. The feeling will get worse before it gets better but stay with it. Don't allow your mind to chatter, and stay with the emotion until it disappears completely.

Check it. Look at the situation again. Make the picture of you in the same situation. How does it make you feel now? Does it evoke feelings *anywhere* in the body? If you find a little residual emotion left somewhere else, look at it. Is the belief behind it true or a product of your mind swindle? Watch that until it disappears too. Keep doing this until there are no feelings attached to it. Sometimes you need to do this once, sometimes a few. It depends on the person and how entrenched the trigger is.

When it goes away completely, it has played itself out. Your neurons have learned to fire differently. You dissolve the need to behave a certain way. You are free of that trigger. You are free to choose to behave a different way. When you arrive at that trigger again, you will feel differently.

Test it. Make a picture of it again. How do you feel now? If it still evokes feelings, what is the belief that drives the feeling? Is it true? Watch the feeling again until it disappears completely. Once you start responding differently you can choose to behave the best way for you now.

Because we have been behaving this way for a time there is probably more than one trigger. We have learned behaviour patterns over and over again. We respond similarly to different stimuli so triggers can (and do) stack up. You may need to look at the same emotional triggers more than once. They may sit in different places within the body. The trick is to become aware of what they are - an automatic response to a given situation. We can eliminate them and learn to act in a different way. You just have to start thinking about *how* you want to act now.

You can congratulate yourself when you overcome the urge to follow the trigger with a pattern response. You can form new positive triggers. Use them to your advantage.

Remind yourself to feel good about your positive changes.

Thoughts Create!

Remember your thoughts create how your body
behaves. Consider your thoughts. How do they
make you feel? If they tell you that you can't do
something, how will you manage to? If they tell
you people do not like you, how will you
respond?

Exercise:
Consider these thoughts one by one. What
chemicals are being made and how would that
make you behave?

"They do not like me."

"I know what's going to happen."

"I can't do this."

"Things normally go wrong for me."

"I will never get over this."

"Sometimes, things can change in an instant."

"There is another way."

"I know what to do."

"Things are going to change."

All these thoughts are beliefs. Some may feel

---

familiar: others may not. Remember beliefs seem 100% correct even if they are not. You have learned them in the past and they control you.

You will learn later how to stop your reaction to these thoughts, but for now you can use the cooling breath. It will help calm you. Have you been practicing breathing into your belly?

Moods

Feelings are your body's chemical reaction to the rest of the world. They create moods and this makes your personality. Your personality controls your behaviour. You cannot feel happy with a lack of serotonin. Instead you will feel depressed.

Creating more positive moods will enhance the production of more positive chemicals. You will start to feel better. If you have previously felt stuck; no wonder you felt down! You had nowhere to go. Now you can see that you have new choices and that realisation in itself will create a more positive mood.

You can start by changing your mood. A mood of optimism – looking forward to changing and what it will mean for you. Start by thinking how things will be. Looking at what you will gain; and pausing long enough to see how you can achieve this will bring about a more positive mood, and will make things so much more achievable.

If you are still unhappy then you are still in a mind swindle somewhere. You believe you can't change; don't want to change; can't imagine a change. And yet you want to. Maybe you feel stuck?

Fundamentally you know somewhere that something isn't right. You want something different.

Why would you look for something different if you do not believe it is going to happen?

You are in a *Catch-22*[11] situation. How can anything change unless you believe it can? When nothing changes, how can you believe it could? This is the point where many of us get stuck and so nothing changes. Your mind swindle continues to fool you into believing that this is the only way. You make excuses for it - reasoning why things don't change. It becomes part of your story.

But in order for something to change, the choices you make need to change – however small.

Instead of seeing what you have always been told, you can start seeing the change. If you give

---

[11] Heller Joseph: Catch 22 (1961)

yourself permission to see how to change things, you actually start to change things. Think about it. Imagine it. Play with the submodalities. Make it as lifelike as you can.

Exercise:
How would it feel to change?

How would life be different?

Take some time to think it through.

How will you respond to people?

How will people respond to you?

How does that make you feel?

Conclusion:

- It is time to start taking responsibility for your own change.

- You cannot change other people - just yourself.

- Changing the way you respond to other people will change their response to you.

- State what you want in positive terms. "I want…"

- A past future loop stops you from

changing the future for fear that nothing will change.

- If you are thinking of the past or worrying about the future and it is affecting you now, it's a past/future loop.

- You will remain stuck if you allow past/future loops to continue.

- Thoughts create feelings.

- Feelings are your chemical reactions to what you believe is happening.

- You respond unconsciously to triggers. Look out for them. Make them conscious. Are they still needed?

- Eliminate triggers. Learn to respond a different way.

- Can it be that simple? You know now how your mind and body work together to trick you into keeping things the same.

- Remember it is doing this because it believes it is for the best. This is your mind swindle.

- What's stopping you from change? You are! Your mind swindles!

- Once you decide how to change, things will start to change.

- Your beliefs skew your perspective.

- Different realities are just other perspectives.

- Perspective sets the stage for *everything*! How you think! How you feel! How you behave. How you respond.

- Beliefs create behaviour - You act the way you *think* you should.

- You always behave with positive intent, even if it doesn't work out that way.

- Question *EVERYTHING!!!*

- Is it true?

Food for thought before you move on:

Is it time for a change? Up until now you have been predisposed to think, feel and behave certain way, and you do so automatically without really thinking about what you are doing.

Without questioning whether this is correct, life will continue as it always has.

PART FOUR

NOW can you see your MIND SWINDLE?

NOW is such a simple concept it shouldn't really need explaining, and yet it does. Now is NOW! This moment. But what is this moment?

Well at this moment you are reading these words. Your eyes scan the paper or screen. Your hands hold the book or electronic device. Your eyes recognise the words. Your fingers make the pages turn. How does it feel to touch the page? You are probably sitting or lying and hopefully relaxing – contemplating this simple subject. Now is this moment.

But where is your mind while you are relaxing here now? Are you contemplating the future or thinking about the past?

What are you doing NOW?

What is your mind doing? Does it wander?

What are your thoughts saying?

What are you feeling?

What are the chemicals driving your body?

What are you responding to? What is happening to you right now?

Do you know why you are feeling like this?

While you are in this moment now, you are responding from the perspective of your past. It is your past that has made you the person you are today. You behave as you do because of your past. It is what you believe to be correct. It is *your truth.*

As you read these words you will respond to them according to your past. You may think this is all very predictable and that you know where I am going; or you may be excited to learn new ideas, eager to read on and see where it leads. It's all dependent on your past and how it has taught you to respond to these things.

What did your past teach you?

How do you respond to this?

So what is NOW? It is a product of your past. A different you with a different past would see the situation differently. They would have a different reality. They would respond differently and the outcome would be different.

If you look back at your history, you know where you have come from. You know why you are here now.

You can see the people who have influenced your life for better or worse. Those who taught you how to think and what to believe. They taught you about the world and your place in it: what to expect from life. Through them, you learned how to respond to the world and so you do that now, without really thinking about it.

You are at this point now, possibly upset about the past - responding to it as though it were happening still. Remember the brain doesn't know the difference between imagination and reality. If you are imagining it, you are responding as though it is still happening.

It was your past that made you believe those things.

It was your past that made you feel those things.

It is your past that makes you do those things.

You may be here NOW but it is your past that dictates what you do now. It is your mind swindle making the same things play out over and over and you respond chemically.

And so to the future... you sit here in the now and predict it. What is going to happen? You are responding physically to what you believe is happening. It doesn't matter what *is* happening. You respond to what you *believe* is happening or what you *imagine* might happen but from a perspective of what's happened in the past and only how you remember it.

NOW ⬅➡ **Future**

Your thoughts bring about a series of chemical reactions and behaviour patterns initiated from your past/future loops and triggers. Have you starting noticing them in your life?

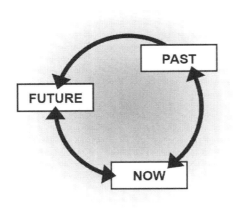

Imagine someone who has had an unhappy relationship. The relationship ends and they are left feeling rejected. How might that affect future relationships?

If something triggers a memory, how might they start to feel? How might it affect their behaviour? How will it affect how the other person feels? If not checked and changed, how might it affect the new relationship?

How we think things will happen, makes us respond in certain ways. What we believe, affects our perspective and behaviour. We unconsciously respond as we know -what we believe is right. We think it is the best course of action without ever questioning if it is, and quite often it is that action that causes the thing we fear. We make things happen with a self-fulfilling prophecy. *'I knew they'd leave me. Everybody does.'*

What is going on? Do you know? Can you guess from what has happened before? Is it imagination? How do you KNOW what will happen? It might happen differently - especially if you do something differently.

If you have had a good life, you will expect more of the same. If you have had an unfortunate life where you've had it tough, why would you expect things to improve for you? You will fully expect things to go wrong. This will determine how you respond to events. Therefore, whilst thinking about the future and what may happen, we behave in the now and this affects the outcome.

Not knowing the future can cause anxiety, a fear of the unknown, so our mind creates a future. We second-guess what is going to happen next. When looking ahead you literally imagine what is to come – what might happen. Your internal monologue tells you. This is unconscious and we do it continuously.

Remember your imagination is run by your thoughts. The brain doesn't know the difference between what is real and what is imagined. Images cause a reaction; they make chemicals and feelings. This is what causes you to behave a certain way. You automatically behave how you have done before - chemically.

The situations in which we find ourselves are a repeat of times before. Our belief systems rarely change so we continue to believe the same and therefore our actions remain the same. The original thought about how to behave is reinforced so lives continue to go round in circles as we learn that *that* is the best way to behave. Your thoughts, feelings and behaviour bring about a certain response.

This is your mind swindle.

Imagine being a rock climber. Rock climbing involves climbing up rock faces where the goal is to reach the summit. Rock climbing is both physically and mentally demanding. It tests a climber's strength, endurance, agility and balance, along with their mental control. How do they manage to climb up rock faces and stay alive? By staying aware of their surroundings – noticing what's around them. In short – living in the now. What would happen if they left the now? If they looked down and became scared they may fall. What if they started to worry what might happen as they climbed further? How would that affect their behaviour? Reaching the summit safely is dependent upon full concentration on *the now*.

Now is such a simple concept. People may think it is obvious, but is it?

Now is this moment, but where is your mind at this moment?

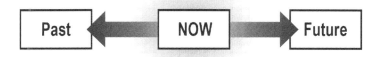

Food for thought:

If you stopped being stressed about what were behind or ahead of you, what would you have to worry about?

If you took the situation and dealt with it as it arose, how would this affect you? Remember the rock climber?

What you imagine might happen, might not happen. It is your imagination that has created that picture.

If you dealt with it when it happened as opposed to being in fear of the fact it might happen, things might be different. You may choose in the moment to behave an entirely different way – if you hadn't already programmed yourself.

What is the worst that can happen? Sometimes we build small things up into huge things. We imagine all sorts. Our bodies respond, chemically and we create behaviour patterns to protect ourselves, even though it doesn't always work out that way.

Clock and psychological time

If this is interpreted as 'do not think about the future', it is a miscommunication. The rock climber *has* to plan how to get to the summit; otherwise they would be climbing over the rock all day!

Life runs along a path and we have the ability to choose how to travel and where we go. Planning for the future is good. The philosopher Eckhart Tolle[12] called this "Clock Time". Clock time to some extent is what we all need. It is actual time – calendars and planning. Clock time is getting to where you are going when you need to be there. From catching a train to knowing what you want to be when you grow up, people need clock time.

---

[12] Eckhart Tolle *The Power of Now* (2005)

Human beings are excellent at forward planning. It sets us apart from other animals. This is how our pattern response works. If I do 'X', 'Y' will happen. We can use this forward planning to our advantage. *'When I grow up, I want to be …'*. Or even just making sure you are on time today. Both are using clock time.

Along with clock time, Eckhart Tolle described another form of time he called psychological time. Stuck in the past or thinking about the future, depending on whether you imagine it to be your saviour; or you're fearful of what it might bring. Psychological time is the past/future loop.

Psychological time is looking into the future and having it stopping you from getting the most out of life now, by worrying about what is going to happen. Psychological time is that situation that makes you unhappy or stressed.

Psychological time is also looking forward to the future with anticipation and expecting life to be in some way better than it is now. *'I may be suffering now but it will be ok later.'* They remain suffering; waiting for their *'now'* to get better of it's own accord, but it doesn't.

Instead of doing anything constructive (clock time) people spend their time worrying in case *it* does or doesn't happen. (Psychological time) *"What if this happens?"* Remember the brain

cannot tell the difference between what is real
and imagined.

*"I do not want **that** to happen."* Remember the
brain does not see the negatives. Sometimes
when you say, *"I don't want that to happen."* It
brings about a pattern of behaviour that *makes* it
happen. You and your behaviour create your
reality.

At times, all the things that we need to do can
feel overwhelming. This is another past/future
loop. Fearing you won't get everything
completed (psychological time). Maybe the
onslaught keeps going and you fear you will
never get to the bottom of your to-do list. The
future appears as hard as the past has been. It
can feel immense and the temptation is to quit. If
you have quit before, you are more likely to quit
again. If in the past, you have learned to keep on
going until the end of your list, you will.

Psychological time is an imagined future. It may
seem real but it is not. The brain doesn't know
the difference between reality and imagination.
It responds in just the same way.

Psychological time stops you from being who
you want to be. It is:
'I am this way because...' (of something that
happened in the past)

'I can't help it because...' (of something that
happened in the past)

'Oh I wish...' (my future would be different)

'I am afraid of...' (because I learned it in the past)

'I need 'X' to make me happy' (I have learned in the past I need this and you look to the future to get it)

'I hope 'X' doesn't happen' (it's happened in the past.)

'I do not want it to happen' (I fear the future)

'What if it does?' (are you imagining the worst future?).

Psychological time is your mind swindle. You believe it's true and respond to it as though it is. It is your mind playing tricks on you. How will it help to let your mind think back to the past or create an imagined future full of worry and anxiety? It is as simple as a thought, and your mind and body behave a certain way, bringing about the conclusion that you were afraid of.

Whenever you feel bad, stressed or depressed you are in your mind swindle. You are in a past/future loop -comparing the past, or worrying about the future.

Stop and breathe for a moment and think about what you can do to make the situation easier? Use clock time. Look at things a different way. Remember the yogic cooling breath and breathe.

Activity:
At this very moment you are safe and nothing bad is happening.

Scan your body. Are there any emotions you *have* to respond to?

Are you worried about what might happen or upset about your past? You are in a past/future loop.

Do you need to respond to this now?

Look at the bigger picture. Do what needs doing now to improve this moment, even if that is just to stop and breathe for a moment.

Stop imagining the worst that could happen. Start thinking how it is best to deal with what is happening now.

Take each moment a step at a time and feel pleased with any achievements.

You are changing the future purely by making the most of now.

FEAR

We may need to deal with emergencies and in such cases we have a tendency then to deal with them well. Your adrenalin works for you, giving you energy and strength to do what you have to. You always hear of courageous people that have dealt with terrifying ordeals and you wonder how they did it. They stayed in the now, taking it moment by moment.

———

There is nothing to fear now. We do not fear what is happening now; we fear the future and what might happen. Fears are all part of your past/future loop. Fear is triggered the same way as every other emotion - a thought: *'What if...'*

It is the images we make and the chemical reactions within our bodies that make us feel as we do. *'It has happened like that before, so it will probably happen like that again'*. We link things together: when 'X' happens 'Y' usually follows it.

Fear spreads throughout our body in a split second before you have time to reason whether the cause is a real worry or a figment of your imagination. From the moment you feel it in your stomach, your body sets off a chemical response to the perceived danger. Unless you reason with it, it will continue building, making you feel worse and worse until you react with fight or flight.

Fears are not always real dangers. Unless there is imminent danger like a lion in front of you, they are likely to be imagined. There is a big difference between coming face to face with a crazy axe-man and imagining one in the local woods. You can make yourself scared by imaging the worst. Remember, FEAR stands for **F**alse **E**vidence **A**cting **R**eal.

FEARS themselves are not real. They are not

actually happening. They are an imaginary future - psychological time. Just because you imagine them to be real, it doesn't mean they are. Until what you fear actually happens; it is only a figment of your imagination, but your mind does not know that. What it imagines *may* happen, stimulates the brain to unconsciously believe it *will* happen and we build the chemicals as though it is *going to* happen. When we are stimulated by adrenaline; everything speeds up and it is easy for our minds to run away with us, before we get a chance to think about whether it's actually worth worrying about. You don't question your mind swindle. You believe it; make reasons to convince yourself that it is true, and uphold it if people question it.

Think of a natural disaster. When a calamity occurs there is no time to think fearful thoughts. You just deal with the emergency at hand. Your body uses fight or flight to get you to a safe position. It is when things start to settle that people may become fearful and start reliving the situation or imagining what *could* have happened (psychological time). At the time of trying to survive, there is only time to think about now.

Exercise:
If you think of a fear, worry or concern you have, does it stem from the past or is it about the future? Or maybe elements of both? (A past

future loop)

Is it happening right at this moment?

Is it going to happen for sure or is it a possible scenario – one of many? Psychological time if you like.

Is your mind swindle so strong that you *know* it will definitely happen?

Could you change the future by acting a different way now? By stepping out of the past/future loop and looking at the problem now, you can choose to act a different way.

How would a different you with a different history behave?

What stops you from acting that way? What are you afraid might happen? Is this real or are you imagining the worst? (Psychological time)

You may need to gain new skills or learn not to respond to triggers, but by stopping and looking at your choices rather than worrying, could you have a different future? What skills would you need?

Use the cooling breath to take time out. If you stop for a moment and think, can you see another way? You can choose whether to go this way.

The trouble is our **fear**s cause us to feel uncomfortable. This is our body making instructions, one of which is adrenaline. We respond the only way we know how -chemically with fight or flight.

You stand and fight – acting with some form of aggression; or run from it to avoid it, you'd rather not think about it. The way that you choose what to do is unconscious. You do what you know – a pattern response. You have always done it that way. You do not stop to consider if you could do it differently. You *believe it's your only choice* - you are wrong. Once you become aware of that, you can choose.

Perhaps now is the time to consider another way?

Beliefs

Most people find themselves trapped. They believe they know why they behave a certain way. They have their reasons and attach themselves to them. *'I am this way because...'* (from the past) It is understandable and gives them some sort of comfort. It is their reality. Making a statement such as *'I am under-confident'* or *'I am scared of spiders'* creates a behaviour pattern. The statement is part of the mind swindle. It has come from the past and limits your behaviour. If you know who you are and how you act, how could you act any other way?

Where does the past exist? Is it still playing out now, or a memory played out by your imagination? Something you can revisit in your mind.

By replaying the past, can you change it or alter the outcome? Horrible things may have happened and you've unconsciously learned from those situations. From that your body knows how to feel and what to do in a certain situation. You can't help it. It's part of your autonomic response system. You do not question it; you simply respond. People feel trapped into behaving a certain way. However just because you behaved that way before, are you tied to that behaviour? It may feel like you are, but *are you?* Do you have to keep reacting the same way? Is what you have learned the only way or just one perspective? If you had a different history, would you be responding another way? Would you see the situation differently? An example here would be victim of abuse. As a friend you would tell them to get away. *RUN!* As the abused, you may feel helpless or even at fault.

Past beliefs have impacted on how you have behaved and in return have impacted on the outcome, usually reinforcing what you believed in the first place. Can you learn now to think, feel and believe something else? Is it possible to change the way that you behave thereby changing your beliefs? The past is set and there is no going back, but the future isn't.

Exercise:
Are the things you learn always correct?

If someone else told you *your* story about a friend of theirs, how would you feel about it?

What would you say?

What advice would you give?

If you took yourself out of the situation, how would you view it from another perspective?

Could you have been mistaken in the first place?

Could your beliefs be wrong?

Different realities

The memory of past events only exists in the mind. The trouble is that you only remember it from one perspective - your own. What you have learned depends on your belief system. Maybe if you had a different history and a different belief system then you would be handling the situation differently now.

If you could take a step back and look at the past, you might see that everyone behaved in response to what they had learned before. The people involved behaved as they did for a reason. It is part of their past and their belief system. That doesn't excuse bad behaviour. The point is that with this knowledge you can *choose* to behave differently now.

Exercise:

Let's take a look at a past event that is causing you problems. Do you remember it now?

What did you learn? What was your belief?

Why did you learn that lesson?

Who were the other person/s involved?

Why did they do what they did?

What did they hope to gain?

Did they get it?

Was their behaviour right?

If you heard this story about someone else from other people (another reality) what would you say?

Were the people correct to teach you that lesson?

Is the lesson correct?

What should have happened? (A different reality)

What would you believe now?

How would you feel now?

How would you behave now?

Now you have looked at it from another perspective, can you start to behave differently now?

Eliminating Past/future loops

Whenever you feel bad or negative, stop and look at why. You are somewhere within a past/future loop. You know you are there because you are second-guessing the future based on what has happened before.

People believe they are tied to the past. A victim to what has happened before, but this is incorrect. In the past you learned something: how to think and how to behave. You have unknowingly been hypnotised into behaving that way. Remember the child that was always told they couldn't do anything right? What were they hypnotized into believing?

When *you* are faced with a certain set of circumstances you are compelled to behave a certain way. If you choose to behave differently you would alter the future, but up until this point, your mind swindle had hidden from you the fact that you even *had* a choice!

As you start paying attention to your triggers, you will notice how situations spark off certain moods and behaviours. This in itself is an unconscious process that you have chosen to become aware of. Just by pausing and becoming aware before you act, can change things.

From there you can decide what to do next – do what you have always done or you can choose to do something different. You gain free will.

Exercise:

Do you second-guess the future because of what has happened in the past?

What have you been hypnotised into believing?

Can you see how up until this point, what you have learned to do in the past has dictated how you behave now?

Can you decide to respond differently now?

You can choose to do what you have always done or you can choose to do something different.

You must rewire your brain to respond differently.

Recognise the situation by becoming aware how it makes you feel. Give it a name. For example, being in a certain persons company may make

---

you feel nervous or on edge.

Stop. Take a cooling breath.

Does it suit you to behave like this still?

You can eliminate these triggers as we did so earlier by stopping and looking at the feeling this situation evokes and allowing the feeling to play out. The instructions are in the appendix at the back.

It is only unconscious behaviour patterns that make you continue to behave this way. Make them conscious.

Choose!

PROBLEMS

By now I would imagine that at this point in the book, you know what you want and you are aware of what you have right now. The difference between the two is your problem.

Why aren't you already the person you want to be? What is stopping you? This is the problem.

'I am this way because...'
'I want to but...'
'If only...'

The *"buts"* and *"becauses"* are your problems.

They are all examples of your mind swindles. It is hard to see around it. It is rationally thought out. It has grown up with you. You have answers for it. You believe it is true because something happened in the past to show (hypnotise) you it was. You have been finding proof that it was true ever since. You believe there is no choice but that belief is wrong.

It is your past future loop stopping you from doing what you want. FEARs are holding you to the same old behaviour patterns. Without your past/future loop you could choose to act a different way.

When thinking about the past or future you believe that you have little choice. This is the belief that holds you to the life you have right now. There is always a choice. You can behave anyway you choose; you just didn't consider it before. Becoming conscious of that fact gives you choice.

Choosing is a part of everyday life we all take for granted. You *choose* to respond the way you do: you just do it unconsciously. Making it conscious means that if you wanted to, you could choose to behave another way. Some of us are really good at choosing, others need more practise. The more you do it, the easier it becomes. You have to consciously decide what it is that you should do instead.

People can feel driven by FEARs into making their choices because they believe they have no other options. Imagining the worst brings a feeling of dread that stops a person from making a different choice and moving on. People running on adrenaline can't see the bigger picture. They remain stuck.

If you stop for a moment you can see why you remain stuck. What is your problem? What do you need to change? How can you do that?

Exercise:
Maybe now is a good time to think about what you need to do in order to change things. If you stop and breathe for a moment the answer may come to you. Remember the cooling breath? Try it.

What is the answer? What do you have to do differently to get a better outcome?

Dare to think about it. Lose your FEARs. It is only your mind swindle playing tricks on you.

Start with the problem. **"I'd like to but…"** This is what you need to change. In order to change how you must be?

Imagine a different way that a different you, with a different history would imagine.
Try something different.

CHOICES

People sometimes forget they have choices. They are so busy thinking about their problem, that they forget they can do something about it.

Remember that thoughts create, so perhaps it is a good time to re-think your problem another way.

Keep the problem

You can choose to keep things as they are. You don't have to choose anything different if you don't want to. Things may continue as they are. They might improve of their own accord in their own time. They might get worse. Only you can make the choice to change.

Maybe you can't change things. For example, the loss of a loved one or deterioration in your health can make change feel impossible. If you truly cannot change things, then you have to learn to come to terms with the situation. Accept it as one of those things – an adversity you have to face. There is little value to twisting yourself up inside because it can't be changed, however much you desire it. What good will it do? Things will still be the same. Learn to deal with it as best you can. Think about different ways to cope with the way things are. Is there more support for you in this situation you don't know about yet? Can you learn to accept things as they are and move on?

With acceptance comes inner peace and an ability to move on from where you are now. You can learn to live with your circumstances. If you fight the situation, you cannot see past your problem so there is little room for movement. You simply remain stuck where you are.

If you are mourning a loss or a change that you cannot do anything about, you will eventually have to do something you don't want to. Accept it.

Sometimes you believe that you cannot do anything about your problem, but this is actually your mind swindle playing tricks on you. You believe that you are stuck in your predicament when actually you are not. These are fear-based predicaments. If you fear the outcome or even think you know the outcome before you try; this is your mind swindle. You have to become conscious of the fact that you have a choice before anything can change.

Change the problem

Some part of you already knows what you must do to change things and how you need to act. So far it has been some fear or concern that has stopped you from changing things. *'What if...'* But fear is just False Evidence Acting Real. It isn't actually true; you just *FEAR* that it might be. It comes from the past and it is about the future - you believe it is true and act upon the fear as though it *is*.

And so you live with the sense of *'what if'*, and nothing changes. You don't try. Maybe you have tried before so what's the point in trying again? It won't change. You know what will happen. And so things remain the same. Up until this point perhaps you didn't know you are more likely to react the same way as before. Maybe you didn't know that most thought and behaviour are unconscious. Perhaps you never thought about, whether what you believed was true or a figment of past learning. Maybe you didn't realise you had a choice to behave another way.

You have simply become used to an old behaviour pattern - a pattern response. If you chose to do things differently, something else might happen. If you continue to do something new, that too becomes automatic and unconscious.

Once you become aware of this, you can become aware of what triggers you into behaving the way you do. Once you see triggers for what they are, you can choose whether to react in the usual way or choose to react differently. Break the cycle by just taking a few deep breaths. Become conscious of the your mind swindle. You can then choose a new, more positive behaviour pattern. Just becoming aware of the moment that a trigger occurs will change the way it affects you. You can be an outsider looking in at your reactions. However you change your reaction, it will change your behaviour. You simply have to be aware of your reaction and start changing it to something that suits you better now.

Exercise:

How does that trigger make you feel? For example; When someone says that it makes me feel *irritated* and then I explode into a rage or when I hear that tone of voice it makes me feel *scared* and I start to panic.

When you feel it, stop take a cooling breath.

Decide what you would want to do differently and set about doing it. Only you can change your direction.

You have to rewire your response.

STOP and take a breath!

Any change makes a difference.

Stop the problem

Life has a tendency to go round in circles. You can try and change things but still you find yourself in the same old behaviour pattern. It can get frustrating. If you have tried to change things and keep arriving back at the same point, you may decide you need to break from the problem completely. What does the problem give you? Does the negatives outweigh the positives? Where are you lacking? What do you need? Where else can you get that? Look within yourself and see.

What stops you from making the break? Before now, your mind swindle did. The triggers, the pattern responses, your past future loops. Living in hope that something or someone else will change; that things will get better on their own. Maybe you didn't even realise that you had a choice up until now.

- If you don't want to accept the situation any more, change.
- If you cannot change things gradually, stop trying.
- If you have had enough, just stop.
- You can accept it didn't work. You can accept you have tried enough times.
- When you accept enough is enough, stop. Leave the problem behind and walk away.
- There is always another choice.

Food for thought:
Once you can see your problem for what it is, you can choose how to react. You are chemically and physically responding to old triggers –

before now, unconsciously. Once you have stopped reacting the way you have always done, you can start acting differently. This behaviour will ripple out into as many areas of your life as you need.

Behaviour always has a purpose. You react this way for a reason. You believed that this was the correct way to act. You can change your mind at any time.

Now

Now we have a better understanding of how the past and future controls our behaviour NOW.

There is safety in what we know and it is comforting to know what to expect, but this also limits us to the confines of our mind swindle. This is what stops us from challenging what we believe.

If a problem concerns another person, they have their own mind swindle. Their own history: their own reality.

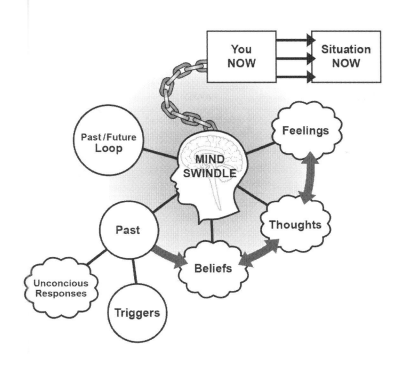

Living in the now is empowering because it allows you to try something different from what you have always done.

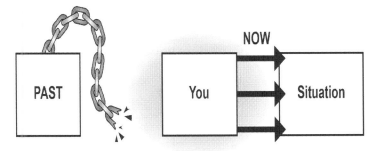

When you live in the now, you can respond in the moment as it happens. You can free yourself from fear of what will happen in the future by using clock time and planning for your future. This can break any cycle of behaviour. As soon as you recognise this past/future loop you can break it.

NOW is what you can do right now. Changing what you can to build a better future.
Just as the prayer by Reinhold Niebuhr goes:

> *Grant me the serenity to accept the things I cannot change, the courage to change the things I can and the wisdom to know the difference.*

NOW is dealing with the rock face right now. If you stop and breathe for a moment you can look and see where you are right now. Get a feel for what is the right way for you to feel better.

People do not like being faced with uncomfortable emotions so they tend to bury them, hidden beneath rhyme and reason. To explain this, they develop attachments to personality traits – *'I am X because...'*. They learn to deal with situations their own way from past experience; given the fact they believe that *'I am X'*.

Other people around us seem to cope so we find ways to cope ourselves. We create actions and behaviours – coping strategies.

Anytime those feelings rear their head, a person responds unconsciously. They learn to deal or cope with them. If you explain them and give them a reason, maybe you won't have to face them.

You have to stop running. Facing uncomfortable feelings and seeing them for what they are, will enable you to free yourself from them. If you are afraid of what is lurking in the shadows, you have to look. Take a deep breath and turn on the light.

Just because you learned to behave a certain way in a given situation, it doesn't mean you have to continue to behave that way. It just takes conscious effort. Without the past holding you back you are free to be anyone that you want to be.

If you are still unhappy then you are still in the past/future loop somewhere. You believe that you can't change or don't want to change; can't imagine a change and yet you want to... otherwise you would not have read this far!

Fundamentally you know somewhere, that something isn't right. You want something to be different.

If you feel stuck, you have not changed your perspective yet. Why would you look for something different if you don't believe it is going to happen? This is a no-win situation. How can anything change unless you believe it can? When you see nothing changing, it is hard to believe it can.

This is the point where many of us get stuck and so nothing changes. But in order to make a difference, something has to change, however small... It has to! It is up to you to do something different. Make a conscious choice to change the problem.

Instead take what you have always been told that "seeing is believing" and turn it on its head. If you start to show yourself that something *can* change, it will. Instead of "seeing is believing", now try believing first and then seeing the change.

Remember the differing realities? What you perceive as real is just your perspective (your mind swindle). But you only see things the way that support your reality. It is a perspective that dates back as long as you do: how you grew up; what you were shown. How you react to everything comes from what you have learned in the past.

If you are stuck, it is because of something you were taught previously either by yourself or someone else. It doesn't mean that what you learned was correct. It just felt correct at the time. Once upon a time, when you were a kid at

Christmas you might have thought it was exciting. Maybe now you are grown up, you have a different view of the festive season. You can change your mind at any time. You can decide that what you thought before is wrong now. There is another way.

Activity:

From the moment *you* start to change, *things* will start to change.

Do you know who you want to be?

Do you know where you want to go in life?

Do you know what you want?

Why aren't you already being that person? What is your problem?

Can you see it as a mind swindle now? A past/future loop?

With conscious effort, you can look at it without FEAR and break free.

It is from this point that you can move forward.

Stop allowing the past to hold you back.

Stop living in fear of the future.

Allow yourself to see a different future.

How will you behave?

However small, you have to start to make the change.

Is *NOW* a good time to start?

Conclusion:

- Now is this moment. Not before: Not after. Simply NOW.

- It is your past that has made you the person you are today.

- You have - until now- been defined by your past and all that you have learned.

- Beliefs about yourself and the situation you find yourself in have also been learned in the past. They are part of your mind swindle.

- Past beliefs limit your behaviour now.

- Replaying past events mean you continue to respond to them.

- You are at this point NOW thinking about your future. Do you FEAR it? Are you worried? Do you hope that things will just improve with time?

- Are you living in this moment NOW?

- Are you in a past future loop? Eliminate them.

- There are two types of time, clock and psychological.

- Clock time is planning. Remember the rock climber?

- The mind swindle is psychological time.

- Do you know what you want now?

- You know what you want and what you have. The difference between the two is your problem.

- Your problem is your mind swindle. It holds you to past learning.

- A different you with a different past, would see things differently.

- There are always three choices: keep the problem, change the problem or stop the problem.

- If you take yourself out of your mind swindle and look at where you are NOW, you'll be able to see what you need to do in order to change things.

- The mind swindle is being afraid to try.

- Now that you have this knowledge, you have free will. You can consciously choose what to do next.

- Now you know all this, things can start to change.

Food for thought before you move on:

Have you been hypnotised into believing certain things because of events that have happened in your past?

Have you been instantly and unconsciously responding the way that you have learned?

Have you been tied to your behaviour by things that have happened in your past?

Does your past dictate how you behave now?

Do you second-guess the future? Are you sure about the outcome?

Can you see your mind swindle now?

How are you feeling now?

PART FIVE

Things that may stop you changing

It is not easy to change things. This may be the first self-help book that you have read, or perhaps you've read lots. People invariably won't succeed in changing their behaviour completely in one go. After all, your behaviour has been built up over a period of time and during that time you have learned how to behave, or at least what you thought was the best way to behave in a certain situation.

Whilst changing, you may be prompted to respond a particular way to an old trigger. It is very easy to find yourself returning to old behaviour patterns. Ways that you used to feel at certain times, or ways you may be inclined to act. These things might stop you from changing.

Once you recognise the patterns for what they are, you can do something about them.

Mistakes

Those times when you do or say the wrong thing. Sometimes you might recognise it as a mistake but other times you might not and you just deal with the consequences.

Even after you see your mind swindle for what it

is and discover the beliefs that you once held are incorrect, it is easy to respond instantly and automatically as you always have. It is only later, when you get a chance to reflect upon the consequences that you think, *'Whoops! That was a mistake!'*

It is easy to make mistakes when you have previously trained yourself to do things a certain way. If you have always behaved a certain way, it is easy to slip back into old habits. At the moment, you are programmed to behave a certain way, unconsciously responding to old triggers.

First of all – you are allowed to make mistakes, everybody makes them. If I claimed to be perfect there would be many people ready to stand up and remind me about the many times that I was not!

Every experience and every situation has the potential to teach us something. What we learn is dependent on how we are feeling and what our belief systems are. Sometimes we have learned the wrong thing. Sometimes we are mistaken. New beliefs are created because of old beliefs. It is not until you recognise the belief is wrong that can you change things. Only then, comes the process of reprogramming yourself to think and behave a different way. If you are used to doing one thing, it isn't easy to just change to doing something else. There are bound to be times when you slip up and revert to type. But unless you recognise the mistake, you will just carry on making it.

Mistakes are fundamental to our learning process. It was Thomas Edison that said before he invented the light bulb, he found 1,000 ways not to invent it. Mistakes are part of the learning process.

We are trained from a young age that mistakes are not good. At school if you make too many mistakes you fail. At school if you make mistakes you can be made to feel like the dunce. This is an incorrect teaching. Mistakes are meant to happen. It is an important part of learning. No inventor ever got it right first time. If Edison hadn't kept trying to get it right, we wouldn't have indoor lighting. Mistakes are a good thing - especially if you are reinventing yourself.

People have a tendency to beat themselves up if they have done something wrong – especially if they are used to doing so. Instead of making it a bad thing, a mistake could be seen as a point in time that made you stop and consider whether you were right. Mistakes are those points in life where people can reflect and learn lessons. We have learned something even if it is simply; *'never do THAT again!'*

In order for you to rectify your mistakes, you first have to acknowledge them.

- Take time to know where you went wrong so you can avoid that path again.

- See how it happened.

- What could you have done instead?

- What have you learned?

- Do what you can to rectify the situation. If you have slipped up it is only fair to do what you can to put it right.

- To put it right you may have to acknowledge your mistakes to others. This might damage your pride or make you behave negatively. You can change this.

- Remember that to the other person, YOU are the situation. They have a different reality to you. They will react the best way they know how. They approach the situation from their past, their reality, and their belief systems. They will react with their own emotions and their own perspective.

- Do what has to be done! Take a deep breath and acknowledge what it is you have to do to in order to break the loop.

- Do it free from fear of what may happen next, and wait to see what does. The loop is then broken and you can choose to behave any way you choose. Just let go of the fear of what may be and deal with things as they happen.

- You are only human; you are doing the best you can.

- If you have no negative feelings you are out of the past/future loop. Well done! You can move on.

Cycles

If you do not learn lessons, the mistakes will happen over and over. You may find yourself in similar situations at other times with other people – the same old behaviour, cropping up again and again. You are stuck with the same behaviour patterns. This is just another example of a pattern response as you find yourself, behaving unconsciously in similar situations - stuck in the past/future loop. Acknowledging this isn't working and changing your behaviour is the only way to break the cycle and therefore change the outcome. Until you acknowledge what you are doing wrong, the situation will persist. This is the first step to putting it right and will break the cycle of behaviour.

Exercise:
Think of a situation that drives a repetitive behaviour pattern. Write it down.

What is the belief that holds you to this behaviour that you haven't yet looked at?

Is the belief correct or a product from your past that isn't true?

Is there an unconscious trigger that you need to become aware of?

What can you do to change the way you behave once you are aware of it?

What other behaviour can you do differently to stop you from doing it again?

What do you need to do?

Could it be that simple?

When you become aware of the triggers, you can teach yourself to respond differently to them.

How do you feel just before you respond to the trigger? Give it a name. Recognise it so next time you feel this way, you will know that the trigger is coming.

Take a deep cooling breath and stop the trigger.

How could you behave differently?

You can choose to behave differently at this point.

Change the behaviour; change the outcome.

Breathe and choose to do something different. The only fear should be things staying the same, so choose what is right for you now.

Guilt

Guilt is really a sub-heading of mistakes. As we've already said, we all make mistakes. It is about learning the lesson and moving on. Feeling guilty can twist you up inside. *'Oh why did I do that?'* *'I wish I hadn't done it!'*. It is no good wishing; you did! Replaying it over and over will just make you feel bad. The mind does know the difference between what is real and what you imagine.

The past has gone and for whatever reason; you did what you did. You made that mistake or maybe several. Your mind swindle made it happen. You were reacting to past teachings, triggers or unconscious responses driven by your beliefs. You did what you felt you had to do at the time and this was powered by chemical reactions and past/future loops. Do you know why you did it? We always do what we believe is the best course of action at the time, even if it turns out to be wrong.

This doesn't absolve you from your behaviour but it does give you a reason. Whatever your reasons, you alone are responsible for your actions now. Actions have consequences. It is now that you can learn from your mistake.

We come to each situation from our own past and our own set of priorities and rules - what we believe is correct. Just because we believed we were correct at the time; doesn't mean to say that it was correct. We can be mistaken. Every one of us can, (and do) make mistakes. It's part of being human.

What happens if you just keep replaying your mistake over and over with regret, but without doing anything to change? It is time to stop going over and over mistakes and start to make the change.

Exercise:
Where does the past actually exist?

Can you turn back time?

Can you change it?

Does going over and over the past change it?

How does it make you feel to keep replaying it?

What chemicals are released?

How does your guilt affect you?

How does it affect those around you?

How would it be if you just mended the mistake as best you could, released yourself from the guilt and did something different from now on?

Can you learn and move on?

You can choose what to do from this moment on.

By staying in the present moment, you will see other options. You can then choose whether to use them. What might you need to change?

Being sorry but not changing things is pointless. Sorry is just a five-letter word. Without change, life goes round in circles and you will soon find yourself in a similar situation: stuck in a past/future loop and reacting to unconscious triggers.

Stop now and see what you can do. It is not about being sorry; it is about changing. Change needs honesty and communication, even if only with yourself; you have to be honest.

What does everyone involved in the situation, need for a better way forward? Is this true or another part of your mind swindle?

You have a choice:

Be unafraid of the future and look for a better now.

Change what can be changed and decide if you can accept the rest.

What do you need to stop this happening again?

Guilt is the regret of mistakes and the wish things were different, but of course, that's impossible. It is what it is.

How you deal with overcoming your guilt is a matter for your own conscience. If you are truly sorry, you will do what you can do to rectify the damage. This means changing your behaviour. Doing what you can to make amends. Ensuring it will never happen again.

When you have done all this you can learn and move on.

For more help, go back to the steps in *Mistakes*

Pride

None of us likes to be proved wrong. We all like to feel that we are in the right but sometimes we have to hold our hands up and take responsibility. It is part of acknowledging our mistakes.

What about those who are too proud to hold their hands up? Where are they coming from?

Do they think they could never make mistakes? Are they really that good?

Do they think they will lose the power they have if they back down? What drives them to act this way? They too have a past/future loop. It is their mind swindle that drives them - unconscious beliefs gained from past learning.

Allowing yourself to make mistakes can be a liberating experience. It gives you a chance to learn and grow.

The saying *'pride comes before a fall'* is usually true. Instead of just backing down when they should; some people tend to go round in circles, tying themselves in knots, just to prove they were right in the first place. Eventually they can't go any further and when they feel stuck they may hold their hands up and rather sheepishly admit it or they might resort to the other tactic of angry outbursts or running away (adrenaline based) to get out of an uncomfortable situation.

If angry outbursts have worked before (past/future loop), they may try that first. One

person changing will alter the reaction.
Everyone is learning new ways.

Some people will never admit they are wrong,
digging their heels in and refusing to admit
anything that may weaken their status. These
people can't learn from their mistakes. They are
doomed to a life of cycles where nothing
changes for them.

You have to choose whether to be a part of the
cycle. You can avoid them, confront them, make
a joke of it or just make them aware that you do
not believe they are always right. It is your
choice as to whether you buy into their belief
and your choice how you react to their mind
swindle. There are other ways. The choices are
yours. But you must first decide what course of
action is available to you.

Exercise:
What does pride do?

How does it make you feel?

How does it make you behave?

What is the unconscious belief that drives it?

Is it true?

Choose what you should do next. Not with fear
about what *might* happen but with a conscious

---

choice in what you believe is the right thing to do.

Watch out for triggers. Take a deep cooling breath and decide what to do next.

Anger

Why do people get angry? Frustration, irritation, miscommunication, fear... Maybe you don't even know why you or others get angry. It just appears to be a build-up of emotions – another pattern response or a past/future loop. Sometimes it's just habitual.

Sometimes people are afraid to communicate properly for fear of what might happen. They leave it and leave it. This can cause all sorts of irrational behaviours, sudden outbursts and unhappiness.

Communication is a key part of our lives. We do it all the time using both verbal and non-verbal forms- either consciously or unconsciously. Even not communicating can be taken as communication by some... from their reality, believing it to mean something.

An argument starts because you have a different viewpoint to another person. You see it from your point of view and they, from theirs. Both parties believe they are in the right and so they are, from their perspective and in their world.

Both could justify themselves to anyone who listens. The trouble is that because of the anger, no one actually listens. All the other person hears is a barrage of words that they then respond to - angrily! Anger triggers an adrenaline-based response. The other person either fights or flights depending on what they are used to doing.

You know what you want and you know what you actually have. The difference between the two is your problem.

How have you and the other person learned to deal with your problems?

How does the argument get resolved?

Does the argument get resolved or does it go round in a cycle? This is another past/future loop or a pattern response. You have to break the cycle and do something different.

Anger can be used as a bullying tactic, by those who have learned that if they shout loud enough; they will get their own way (another past/future loop). You don't have to put up with bullying behaviour but because of what you have learned (pattern response), you may decide that it is your best option. If you were a different you who had learned a different way of life, you might not accept it. If you were a different you who had more confidence, you may choose to break the cycle you are in.

Whether it's you or not, when a person communicates with anger; the other person feels under attack and automatically makes adrenaline. Responding with either fear or aggression – the fight or flight response. The way they react isn't consciously thought about. They respond as they know. Before anger comes irritation. You feel it in the pit of your stomach (it's shutting down) and you feel it in your head. You need to stop it right there before it explodes. Stop and take a cooling breathe. Think about the best way to explain what you need to. Maybe it's hard to think straight so take time to breathe. You will be able to communicate much more effectively. The way to move forward is to break that response and reaction by *NOT* reacting as you always do. Changing your reaction will change the response. See the difference!

You have to break the cycle and communicate effectively. This isn't easy when you are being shouted at or blamed. Still, you can breathe through it and not respond. The trick is to communicate your discontentment before the time it becomes intolerable. Once it's intolerable, it is too late. Your annoyance is obvious and the other person feels attacked and can't help but react. Speaking before it becomes an issue will allow you to have a proper conversation about it. Say what's on your mind without raising your voice or before you feel under threat.

Do you have a solution to the problem?

Sometimes people will go on about what's wrong, but they don't know how to put it right. How can the other person solve this? They may not have the solution. They might just hear *'You're doing this wrong, you're doing that wrong'* and feel threatened. Reframe the statement and say it with positive intention. You can both listen to what the other person is saying. *'When you do that it makes me feel like this because...'.* Hear their reasons. They are coming at this from their perspective or their reality. See if what they are saying is valid. Learn to communicate effectively. *'Could you behave...'* or *'might it work better if you behaved like this...'.* Stop a person from hearing what they are doing wrong; give them a positive instruction how it might be done better; remove the element of personal attack.

How do you feel about what they say? What is your reality of the subject?

This doesn't mean they have to be right but if you stop and listen, they in turn should listen to you too. Change your response.

To resolve your differences, communicate properly. Stop and look at what is wrong, listen to what the other person is trying to communicate. Think about what the other person is saying and the best way to put your point of view across, without making the other person feel attacked.

Some people don't communicate. They are too busy being right or in other words, too proud or stubborn. You can choose to act a different way. Only you know what is right for you.

Exercise:
Take some cooling breaths.

Think before you speak.

What is the best way to get your point across without adrenalising you or the other person?

Don't attack with negative criticism.

Use positive instruction.

Abuse

In some relationships, angry behaviour is more than just angry outbursts or niggling behaviour. The cycle of behaviour is more ominous. There are angry or abusive outbursts where one person is left feeling bad about themselves. This may be followed with apologies or excuses for the bad behaviour.

The bad behaviour is forgiven though the effects of the behaviour remain. Triggers for behaviour have been unconsciously built. Both the abuser and the abused have learned something about the other person and themselves – even if it is unconscious. After a period of settling, the abuser's mood begins to build again and the abused person is left nervously awaiting the outburst that is sure to follow (past/future loop).

The outburst occurs, followed possibly by another apology and excuse for the behaviour.

The abusive behaviour lowers the abused person's self-esteem. They may be blamed for the behaviour or think if they try harder to please, the behaviour will stop. Usually it doesn't. The cycle continues until the person stops their abuser. Maybe they are promised it won't happen again, maybe the abused person is just happy it has stopped for now. The behaviour once again is forgiven but not forgotten, because the same triggers and the expectation that it will happen again makes the cycle continue.

The abuser is coming to the situation from their own past, own beliefs and behaviour patterns. What they have learned and how they believe they should behave. They are part of their own past/future loop. Behaving how they have learned to – most likely unconsciously.

Abusive behaviour may stop for a while but inevitably the cycle continues until the abused puts a stop to it, permanently. The longer the abuse continues, the stronger the triggers and the more helpless the abused feels to stop it.

The lowering of self-esteem and the belief that it will always be like this, and that they are trapped; or the hope it will be different this time (psychological time), always holds them to accept the abuse.

Biologically speaking, this is maintained by a certain combination of chemicals that run through the body. They tell the body how to behave. You can't feel happy when your body is feeling scared. You can't feel strong if you have been worn down to the point of always feeling weak. This is the mind swindle stopping a person from moving on in terrible circumstances. They literally feel trapped.

One of the functions of adrenaline is to stop the stomach from working. It is a non-essential system that isn't needed when fighting or running. Serotonin is one of the main chemicals connected with happiness. Its precursor is tryptophan. This is ingested in some of the foods we eat and made into serotonin in the stomach. As such, when the body is producing adrenaline it stops producing serotonin. You no longer have the feel-good factor and depression takes hold.

Your body starts a cycle of flooding and desensitising receptors with adrenaline. You find yourself in the same moods and acting the same way. It just becomes a habit and the constant flood of adrenaline and the waiting for another attack inhibits you from believing that there could be another way.

This is all run by your belief system, reinforced by triggers. A chemical is released. You are reminded how to act. Unconscious of the biological entrapment, a person will remain stuck until they themselves break the cycle.

The body makes more and more adrenaline until it can't make any more. At that point, the body crashes and you are left with temporary adrenal failure. Depression sets in and you are stuck believing things have to remain as they are. This is the result of the combination of dominant chemicals that control your body.

Food for thought:
Becoming aware of why you feel helpless empowers you to think and act a different way. You become free. You've taken the first step. You know what it is that you have to do.

If this were a friend what would you say? Would you want them to put up with this behaviour?

Get help! There is support out there if you need it.

This behaviour will continue, probably getting worse until you stop it. How long do you want it

---

to continue?

Are they going to stop on their own? Why would they? This behaviour suits them. What do they gain from it?

What do you?

What do you lose?

If you feel abused or trapped, tell someone. Get Support. Change things!

Emotional distress

Anxiety, worry and fear; these popular words are used when you feel emotional distress. Emotional distress is triggered by replaying events that upset you in the past, and worrying about what *might* happen in the future. The brain doesn't know the difference between imagination and reality so it makes the same chemicals regardless. We all suffer from this occasionally, but what happens when you keep repeating these thoughts? Your body quickly gets used to feeling like this. Unconsciously it becomes a habit.

When your body is running on adrenaline it is on high alert. It looks for danger and if you are used to worrying then your body sees it everywhere. *'What if this or that?'* The mind creates pictures and you feel emotional distress.

The hypothalamus, which is part of the stress response, is also in charge of your body's natural balance. If it is used to topping up lots of adrenaline and will continue to make it.

Remember for those who suffer with feelings of emotional distress regularly, there is no cut-off switch so the adrenaline will keep building until it can't build anymore, at which point they will go into adrenal failure and you will feel depressed. Perhaps even catatonic as you usually have high levels of adrenaline spurring you on and without it, you just don't have the energy to move.

It all becomes a cycle. Adrenaline is addictive. Adrenaline junkies get endorphins with their adrenaline. People who suffer with emotional distress do not. The need for adrenaline just gets higher and they encounter more ways to feel emotional distress. Do you find that life can be bit of a drama? You may be in this cycle.

Exercise:
Do you suffer with emotional distress?

Have you got yourself into this cycle of worry or making drama?

Adrenaline is addictive.

Stop and breathe. Remember the Cooling breath in the introduction. Practice it often.

Once you are calmer you can see if your mind swindle is playing tricks on you.

Are you in a past/future loop?

Are you are making **F**alse **E**vidence **A**cting **R**eal?

Is it *going* to happen or can you take steps to change things?

Use clock time. What can you do to make a better outcome for yourself?

Take some time to stop and breathe and think about the situation without FEAR.

Grief

Grief is emotional distress stemming from a great personal loss. It is a wish that things could be different to how they are.

Some may say NOW could not possibly help with grief. Time is the greatest healer. This is true, not only could you not dance a jig when you are experiencing grief, but neither would you want to.

Grief is something that can't be changed overnight. When a loss is experienced there is a hole in a person's life that can't be easily filled or ignored. Grief lessens with time. It is the process we go through in order to lose the attachment to something or someone important to us. There are five stages to the grieving process that a person must go through:

- **Denial** that the loss is happening or has happened.
- **Anger** or resentment for the loss.
- **Bargaining** in order to get back what you have lost.
- **Depression** that it has happened.
- **Acceptance** that it has happened and the ability to start moving on.

These stages do not have to be in that order and a person may go through the same stage more than once, especially if they are stuck in a cycle. They may develop coping strategies to deal with the pain but hopefully, eventually they will come to terms with their loss.

Allow your grief to be expressed. Recognise it as good for the healing process and move on when you are ready. You may experience triggers where your grief is stronger. Acknowledge where they come from. Remember the memory. Grieve as you have to. Then move on with your day. It will lessen with time.

Holding on to grief however isn't constructive, being stuck in any one of the grieving stages or holding on to the first four. This might stem from not being able to accept that things have changed, or regrets about how you have acted in the past. It is as it is. If you can't change things, you have to learn to accept them and let things go. Holding on to something you can't change will only lead to more emotional distress.

Knowing that it is too late to correct your mistakes can cause great distress. Guilt, grief or anger at yourself, (or at another person) can cause a torrent of emotion. However if circumstances are such that you have made mistakes that you can't rectify now, you must accept that they have already been made. The mistakes were not made in isolation; they were likely a build-up of various other circumstances. You can't revisit the past and change things, however much you twist yourself up inside.

Holding onto the pain will not help the pain. Experience it as an emotion but know there isn't anything you can to do alter the situation. Do not allow the mind to chatter with *'what if'* and *'I wish'* because this won't help. Allow yourself to feel the emotional response and, after it's spent, begin to move on. See eliminating triggers in the appendix.

If the person was still around, perhaps you would still be reacting to the same old triggers and nothing much would have changed. It is the knowledge that you can no longer change things that makes it more painful. If the loss is a partner, accepting that *that* was the relationship, and that a relationship takes two, will allow you to move on. Allow yourself the chance to see things from other perspectives.

Learning from your mistakes for the future is the only gain from the situation. Really looking at your mistakes and gaining knowledge from them may help you in the present and will certainly help you in the future. Who knows what the future brings? You may be glad that you learned what you have.

Wishing the situation were different when it can be no other way is time consuming and serves no purpose. It stops you from moving on with your life. Being unable to let go, or holding on to regrets helps no one – not you or anyone else. Fix what can be fixed, accept things that can't. Learn from the experience and let go. (See Guilt)

Seeing what you need to do and letting go can be painful but necessary. Remember good times, let go of the bad. Move on.

Jealousy

Jealousy is that little green-eyed monster that most of us have experienced at one time or another. We may feel resentment or fear that someone is more advantaged than us or feel suspicion of rivalry or unfaithfulness.

In order for any relationship to survive, it needs the foundations of respect and trust on both sides. To be true to the relationship, trust means that you believe what the other person says. A relationship that doesn't have these things has nothing.

Jealousy comes from fear that you may lose what you have now. That you may not be good enough to hold onto it or that someone else might take it away. Is this real or is your mind swindle playing tricks on you?

Look at the relationship honestly. Do you think this is a possibility? Is it part of your mind swindle? Your belief system tells you it is true. If you do not think much of yourself then it stands to reason that someone can take it from you, but take a closer look at the situation. Is it actually happening or is it what you FEAR might happen?

If you stop and look at all the facts, you will actually face your FEARs. See if they have any validity. If they do, then you must look honestly at the reasons why.

Real jealousy is a form of emotional distress so you may want to go back and re-read that section.

Things to consider:
What is jealousy doing to you?

What beliefs are running your mind swindle?

How do they make you feel?

How do they make you act?

What is it doing to your relationship?

Are your FEARs founded or do they stem from your own insecurities?

Where did your insecurities come from?

Where did you learn them?

Is the belief true or part of a mind swindle?

Know what you have to do to stop the cycle.

Self-Respect

Self-respect is having self-worth. To know and value the type of person you are. To like yourself and who you have become. Self-respect is something that many people lack. Even those who may appear really confident can be lacking in self-respect, hiding their self-loathing behind bravado. But even for them, their feelings are made apparent by their self-destructive behaviour.

It is the thoughts about yourself that you unconsciously listen to. Your thoughts shape your behaviour. If you have self-respect then you would like yourself and your thoughts would reflect this, as would your actions. You would be comfortable chatting and meeting new people, safe in the knowledge that you are likable and worthy of people's time. A lack of self-respect would mean the opposite. That little voice in your head could be telling you that people do not like you; that you are not interesting; that you have to behave a certain way to be accepted or that you can never be you. Since it is these thoughts that your body is reacting to, your body is flooded with negative instructions and you behave as you always do – negatively.

Where does this lack of self-respect come from? Where in the past did you learn it? Where did you first learn that you were not likeable or worth knowing? Somewhere in the past this is what you were taught. Once you start thinking like this, you also get feelings like this and once you start feeling like this, you behave like this. Your mind swindle continues to make this a truth and you behave as though it is.

If you stop and think about it, is it true? What type of person are you? How would other people describe you? Step back and look for a moment. It may be hard for you to contemplate how others would describe you. It is your mind swindle trying to pull the wool over your eyes.

Whilst the core *you* remains the same; you probably behave differently around different sets of people. Your friends; your family; your loved-ones; colleagues; peer group - do you know what you get from each relationship? Do you know what they get? Why do they want you in their lives?

When a person lacks self-respect, what others think of them is very important. It gives them their sense of self-worth and so they behave a certain way to gain acceptance from the people around them, even if it doesn't always fit with their moral compass. They are seeking respect from others and not from within. Because of the thoughts that run around their head they behave a certain way. It is the way they act that causes people to react.

The way you act will either draw people towards you or drive them away from you. So if you believe a person might not like you, you will behave in a certain manner (thoughts create). This will probably cause the person in question to give you a wide berth or allow them to treat you as they want for their own gain. If you believe that you are a nice person to be around, you will react differently and because of this more people will be drawn towards you, proving yourself right. It is your behaviour patterns that determine others' reaction to you.

Your behaviour patterns have come from your past and what you have already learned. What did the past teach you?

Exercise:

What kind of a person are you? Do you know?

You probably have more different personality traits than you can think of.

What is your best friend like? Describe them. Write down their attributes you like. We tend to gravitate towards people like ourselves. Chances are; they are someone like you.

Which of those personality traits do you recognise in yourself?

How would your best friend describe you? They know you well. What good points would they list? Write them down and look at them.

Have you ever thought of yourself like this before?

Do the things that you don't like about yourself really matter?

What would you like to change? Once you become aware of what drives the unwanted behaviour, you can change it.

Take another look at yourself...

Your perception comes from what you have learned in the past. Is it all true?

Look at the description of yourself. Are you a better person than you imagined?

How do you feel about that?

Should you start being as kind to yourself as you are to others?

Do you deserve it?

If you don't think you do, look again at the belief. Is it true or your mind swindle playing tricks on you? Repeat this exercise.

Being negative about yourself breeds more negativity. To keep telling yourself bad things will not help. *'I hate being like that'* will not make you any better. Communicate with your mind more effectively. Look for the positive intention. Target areas for improvement. *'I would like to be more like this'* gives your mind something positive to work towards.

Focusing on who you *want* to be rather than who you *don't* will help to bring the positive change about. It doesn't matter who you have been, that is the past (psychological time). That time has passed. What is important now and who you are striving to be in the future. It is only clock time that matters.

Recognise the good bits about you. People without self-respect will find it very unnatural to

178

say nice things about themselves. Some people might even think it was boasting to say good things about themselves, but is it really? If I say that I am a good person, am I boasting? I am also kind, generous and warm hearted. Am I showing off? It's just knowing who I am. It's okay to acknowledge your good points, they are there. They are what the people around you see.

It's okay to love yourself. If it feels strange to say *'I like THIS about me'*, then you need to look at *why* it feels strange. If you can say nice things about others, it's okay to say nice things about yourself. Self-compliments won't go to your head unless you let them. Being arrogant is different. Being arrogant means you are over bearing. Knowing you are good or kind is ok. They are positive traits to be.

Forgive yourself for past mistakes. Remember the mistakes section. Mistakes are allowed. Everyone in the world is guilty of making mistakes. Beating yourself up about them does nothing but make you feel bad. If you think about it, you didn't know then what you know now. You were running unconscious programs triggered by what you had already learned. You had no choice but to behave that way. If you had been able to make a choice, how *could* you have behaved? Once you've identified that, you can strive towards doing that next time. Keep working towards the person that you want to be and you *will* get there eventually.

Comparing yourself to others will simply make you feel bad. You are an individual with positives and negatives, and so are other people. They may be really confident for example, but perhaps they don't treat people as well as you do. If you have trained yourself to see your negative personality traits, take some time to look at your positive ones. Take time to think about them. How do they make you feel?

How do you respect other people? Do you listen to others and hear what they have to say? Do you consider their opinion?

Perhaps it is time to offer yourself the same courtesy. Listen to yourself. Your wants, needs and desires matter as much as everyone else's. It's only your past that has taught you otherwise.

Respect yourself. Negative thoughts continue a negative thought pattern and become a cycle. You are trying to become a better person. Just like you would encourage a child to learn, encourage yourself and see the change in how you feel and what you do. Be kind to yourself. You are like *you* are because of your past, but you do not have to stay that way. It just takes time to learn. When you notice that you are being negative towards yourself, *STOP*. Check yourself and turn the negative into a positive change, however small. Try it.

Don't do something you will later regret simply because you feel you should. You will end up feeling much worse than if you had just stopped yourself responding like this in the first place. If you stop yourself from responding in a way that you normally would, be proud of yourself. Notice how you are changing.

Become conscious of your actions. Admit when you are wrong. Forgive yourself and take steps to change. Congratulate yourself when you do. You are learning.

Activity:
If you have realised your beliefs about yourself are wrong, you can change. You *are* who you *believe* you are. You can act anyway that feels right and be anyone that you choose. You just have to choose and learn. If you have learned one way perhaps it is time to learn another.

Are you fundamentally a good or bad person?

Look at yourself from other perspectives. If your personality traits are good traits to have, it stands to reason you are a good person. How do you feel about the person you are?

Perhaps looking at yourself from other perspectives will allow you to see yourself a different way. Could you like yourself more?

Are you worth knowing? Now that you take

---

time to look, are you a better person than you realised? Would *you* want you as a friend? Maybe this is a good place to start.

Confidence

In order to change things, you have to have the confidence to try. A lack of confidence makes you believe you can't change, or maybe makes you fear what will happen if you dare. The self-fulfilling prophecy comes true: nothing changes.

Having confidence is having belief in yourself, in your strengths and abilities. A lack of confidence comes from the past - what you were taught and what you have learned.

'Child A' is brought up by their family who teach them they are wonderful. They can achieve anything they set their mind to. They are encouraged to try new things and learn from mistakes. They will grow up unafraid to try. They talk openly to people and grow up confident in their abilities.

'Child Z' on the other hand is brought up with inattentive, unsupportive parents. They shout at them and tell them to be quiet. They don't encourage them and make scathing remarks about their abilities. They warn them of how they might fail if they do try. *"You won't be able to do that!"*

'Child Z' will grow up completely different to 'Child A', having a completely different outlook and belief system. If you have never known that you could achieve things, why would you try? If the most important people in your childhood treated you like you were unimportant, why would you think otherwise?

You grow up believing what you have been taught by significant people. They don't even have to explicitly tell you that you're useless for you to pick up the message. The child only has to feel and think it for them to start believing and behaving as if it were true.

What you believe about yourself is therefore dependent on your upbringing. If you had a different upbringing from the one you *actually* had; you would now have a different reality. You have simply been taught the wrong thing. Learn a different way and move on.

Activity:
Did you learn to be confident or under confident?

How did you learn that?

Awareness

While all these things may stop you from changing your life, what *really* stops you is a lack of awareness that things *can* change. Up until this point you have labelled yourself the way that you do because you have given yourself reasons; you are programmed to continue as you always did. It is all very logical. It is your mind swindle working.

You have been taught (hypnotised) what to think and how to feel in certain situations. This all supports your belief system. It is your beliefs that control your whole programming– your thoughts, your emotional and chemical responses and your behaviour. It is because people do not question their belief system that they continue doing the same thing and continue with the same cycles over and over.

'I am X because of Y,' leaves very little room for manoeuvre. How could you be 'A'? Being 'A' has been unthinkable. You would not know how. You have always been 'X'. You are 'X' because of your mind swindles and your past/future loop. You will continue to be 'X' until you take steps to change.

You need to be aware that you can be whoever you want, and learning what that means. Learn how you might behave differently in situations and be ready to learn from the times when you make mistakes and fall back into old habits. Learn how it might feel to behave a different way to that which you have known before. Staying aware that you are changing takes time. Becoming different is a work in progress. How many years did it take to make *you* as you are? It is unlikely to be perfect overnight.

Try something different and as things start to change you will see the difference. You have to undo your mind swindles and make yourself the person you want to be. You can do it if you if *believe* you can. Dare to try!

Conclusion

- There are so many things that might stop you from changing. The odds seem stacked against you, which is why so many people don't. (However, they may not have read this book!)

- At the moment you are chemically programmed to respond the way you do. This is not your fault. It is your history.

- Everyone makes mistakes. Recognise them. Correct them. Move on.

- You may struggle with some form of emotional distress. This is habitual and is the body's addiction to adrenaline. Stop and breathe. Recognise your mind swindle.

- Even the thought of changing can seem scary. This is a past/future loop.

- You might create scary images of what may happen if you try. If create images, your body will respond to them automatically without conscious thought.

- If you don't stop and look at your fears, you will never be able to change.

- Looking at what is stopping you will actually seem less scary once you take away your **past/future loop**. You can change the future by changing the way you behave today.

- In the past, you have learned to have low self-worth. This is your mind swindle. Look at your friends. Their personalities are a reflection about you.

- In the past, you have learned not to have the confidence to try. This is your mind swindle.

- Eliminate past/future loops.

- Remember your thoughts create.

- Becoming aware will help you recognise what is happening.

- Being aware will change the way you feel.

- Staying aware will help you question if this is the way that you *want* to behave.

Food for thought before you move on:

You can now see that every sub-heading essentially covers the same things. What stops you from changing? You do!

Your thoughts tell you something. Thoughts run around your head every waking moment without you ever really noticing them. They come from your beliefs.

Even though you do not stop to consider these thoughts, they continue to make you feel a certain way.

They are literally unconsciously creating a chemical response. The chemicals that drive your body; your beliefs about what you should do and the triggers to which you have learned to respond to are driving you on, making you feel and behave a certain way - unconsciously and without questioning.
This is your mind swindle.

By looking at your mind swindle - your thoughts, your feelings, your fears - you can see if these are *actually true* or if it's your mind swindle playing tricks on you.

PART SIX

Decide NOW What Comes Next

The more I work with people, the more I realise that it is only NOW that really matters. It is your mind swindle that keeps you behaving a certain way. It makes you believe that *it* is the best way: the only way!

The mind swindle is a system that keeps you behaving as you do. You see it everywhere. You feel it always. You respond to it unquestioningly. The mind swindle is the product of everything that has ever happened to you. How you *perceive* it to have happened to you. Your mind is like a computer and has been programmed to believe certain truths.

These truths are absolute. Everything you see, hear, smell, taste and feel reinforces these truths. The mind can only take notice of approximately 7 things at any one time so it ignores anything that doesn't fit with what it believes. It isn't conscious. You don't consciously choose; it just ignores anything that doesn't fit with what you believe.

Twinkle Twinkle Little Star, what you say is what you are...

'I believe I am...(good, bad, horrible, nice)'

'I believe everything is my fault.'
'I believe I am unlikeable.'

These beliefs control your thoughts, your feelings and your behaviour now, but you learned them in the past. Just because you learned them in the past, it doesn't mean that they are true.

Without our past conditioning us, we can be anybody we choose to be. What stops us is the belief that we can't or to put it in more positive terms, the unawareness that we can. Your mind swindle has been ignoring anything that gives you another choice. The first step is becoming aware that the mind swindle is there and that up until now *it* has been controlling everything you do.

"I believe I am a good person."
'I believe that I deserve to be happy.'
"I believe I can change."

So what's next for you? Continue on the same path and see where it leads? Perhaps you feel it's time to change direction? Do you want to try a different way?

The first step to change is altering your perspective. You will have to change your belief systems, thought patterns, behaviours and responses. It can be done. It's just consciously learning another way.

If you are continuing to suffer any kind of emotional distress then you are not in *the now*. You are thinking about your past or worrying about the future. Can you see the past/future loop? Are you expecting the future to be the same as it has been in the past? Guess what? It will be because you aren't changing anything. You are not looking forward to a different future. Only *you* have the power to change things now.

Remember there are two different types of time: psychological time and clock time. Psychological time is your negative thought patterns that relate to a time that isn't now. The *'I wish…'* and the *'What if…'*. Psychological time is regrets about the past, wishing it hadn't happened that way and wanting things to be different. It is also anxiety about the future or waiting for the future to make things better.

Psychological time is an imaginary time and is only playing in *your* head. The future isn't set and can be changed by altering things now. The future you dread may never happen. You believe it might and imagine it to be real.

However sure you are it will play out that way; you can never be certain. The feelings it evokes and the actions that you take may make it more likely to be so, but if you changed how you behave now, it would change your future.

The past however is unchangeable. It has already happened and is only happening now in the mind, re-lived by the imagination that triggers an unconscious chemical response. It can't be changed and what's done is done. How you choose to respond is up to you. You can choose to continue to go over it, again and again. This makes you feel bad chemically or you can learn from it, take a deep cooling breath and start to move on.

The future can be changed but not through anxiety or worry. This will only make you feel bad and stop you changing. What will change things are clock time and an awareness of what needs to be done; what you need to learn and the person you want to become. The future cannot be changed in the future. It can only be changed now with awareness and using *clock time* to plan how you achieve your goals. Start changing things step by step at your own pace, with less fear about whether you can achieve your goals.

So how do you stay in the now? By staying aware of how you are feeling. Surprisingly it isn't that easy initially. Whenever you are feeling bad, you are not in the now. If you take time to look, you'll see you are in a mind swindle. It is made from your past/future loop and behaviour patterns that you have spent a long time nurturing. Most people don't take time to notice them but this is exactly why the swindle is perpetuated.

Only you can choose if you want to stay in the cycle that you find yourself in. Once you see it, you can decide.

Different realities

Remember that you have been taught to behave this way. In your reality, you believed it was the correct thing to do because of what the people around you had taught you.

Exercise:
Who taught you to think, feel and behave as you do?

How did they teach you to believe that?

Why did they teach you that?

What did they have to gain?

How did they teach you to feel?

How did it make you behave?

Were they correct?

If you took yourself out of this situation and heard this story about someone else, how would you respond? Would you feel differently if someone else were the victim of that behaviour?

If it's not okay for someone else to be treated like that, what about you? Is it okay for you to be treated this way?

Is your mind swindle stopping you from seeing that it is not okay for you to be treated that way too?

Do you deserve the same treatment as everyone else?

If you could take away what you were taught, might you believe that you were as good as everyone else?

Has your mind swindle been playing tricks on you all this time?

How do you feel about this?

Now you can choose whether your beliefs are correct, and you can choose what to do about them.

Choices

When you free yourself from what you were taught in the past, you can choose another way. Perhaps you've reached a point where you see that life goes round in circles. You recognise that you have been here before. You have a tendency to do the same thing over and over or even if you do try to change things, you still seem to

193

end up in the same place.

You know now it is your mind swindle that makes it happen this way. Because of your past, you are predetermined to think, feel and act a certain way without conscious thought as to whether it is correct.

Now you have this knowledge, what do you do next? You have three choices.

Keep the cycle
Make a spiral
Break the cycle

Before you decide what to do, now is the perfect time to stop and look at your choices.

Keep the cycle

Keeping the cycle might be seen as the easy option. The outcome is that you stay as you are. You accept your situation as *one of those things*; a cross you have to bear. Unavoidable – unchangeable even! You are always busy reasoning why you are in this predicament. Maybe you just feel stuck.

It is a past/future loop. Instead of using it to see into the future, stop now and decide if you can accept the future as it is.

Will this behaviour get better of its own accord?

Can it get any worse? Stop now and decide if you're okay with that. If you choose to keep the behaviour or feel that you can't change it yet, then is it right for you now?

Whatever you decide to do, you are free to change your mind and your behaviour at any time. This is the beauty of *now*; it changes all the time along with you.

You may believe you know what will happen if you try and change but this is your mind swindle. You are in a past/future loop and imagining the future.

Until you *do* decide to change things, then the best you can hope for is more of the same cycle but again; you can change your mind at any time.

You can't change other people, only yourself, and if your cycle is of use to others, they will be looking to maintain the status quo. We all work with positive intention -that is to say we are trying to achieve something. It is you that has the power to change things now and this is by changing something within that cycle.

There are of course, things that can't be changed, (the death of a loved one, or a disability). If it can't be changed, the answer is to come to terms with it. Accept it and learn to live with it. You'll find it hard to come to terms with at first, but once you do your grieving changes. You will be able to begin to move on. Change things. Make a spiral.

Make a spiral

Changing from A-Z in one fell swoop may seem insurmountable. Maybe it is, but any change in behaviour will change things within the cycle. The cycle is broken momentarily and there is a chance for you to make a spiral. Do something different.

A spiral is a conscious choice to act a different way. To create a different outcome to the one that happened in the past ... even just once.

What would you do if you weren't afraid to try?

Every action has a purpose and if what you are doing isn't working, changing what you do might. You will have a different outcome. Try it and see.

New behaviour patterns have the ability to spiral you upward towards a more positive behaviour or downward towards a more negative one. What you learn from each situation is dependent on your belief system. This can dictate which way you spiral.

If your new behaviour pattern isn't doing what you had intended it to do, you can refine it. You are allowed to make mistakes. Any change will alter the pattern response so a new trigger will remind you how to behave – old ways or new ways. If you start the ball rolling and make little changes, this will eventually lead to larger changes, preferably spiralling up towards a more positive behaviour.

Complete change won't happen overnight – and not just you but also the rest of the world, will have to get used to the new and improved *you*. You can use clock time to plan for a better future. Each time you change something within the cycle, you change the outcome. As you are working towards something positive, enjoy the benefits of the changes. Be happy for small victories. You have worked for them!

Break the cycle

Sometimes little changes aren't enough. There needs to be a drastic one. Now you may see the cycle for what it is and decide you have had enough. It's okay to choose this. Stop the behaviour from happening; give up; cut your losses and walk away.

Sometimes we reach a point at which we say that we have had enough. That we can't try any more. We usually see a break like this coming. It is the result of being aggrieved by the situation for long enough. When the negatives outweigh the positives, it is time to choose another way.

It can seem like the most daunting thing, which is why you haven't changed things so far, but when you reach that point; you will know that changing is your best option. If you can't accept it and you can't alter things, what other choice do you have? You can go round the cycle again or you can stop it by doing something different.

You can continue to complain about it. Live in fear of it. Worry that it can't be changed. All these things *change* nothing.

The same thoughts are created, reinforcing old beliefs. The same chemicals are made reinforcing old behaviour patterns. Life remains the same. The cycle continues.

If something or someone is causing you more heartache than good feelings, and you feel powerless to stop it, walk away.

If you believed it was of some benefit to you, then realise you were mistaken: put a stop to it.

When you have had enough of trying to change things, stop. Look at other possibilities. There are always other choices if you start to look.

Whatever it is you need to do, take a breath and do it, then move on. What is your alternative? You will change the path your life is following and open up new possibilities.

Since other people are involved in your life, there will be a period of adjustment; learning that this is the new way. They may not want this new way but you have to do what is right for you. They may trigger responses in you. There will be chemicals running round your body that make you feel a certain way. You may feel you *should* act a certain way. Is it for the best? Your mind swindle is tricking you; making you see your problems *it's* way. To your mind swindle, there is no other way. It is part of your story. The way you have always seen it. STOP! It can be another way.

Keep reminding yourself why you've decided to change and that this is for the best. You will come through the other side stronger than you went in, because you will know then that change is possible.

Conclusion

- At this moment you are unconsciously, biologically and behaviourally perpetuating your problem. This is your mind swindle. If you stop for a moment you'll be able to see your choices and decide what is best for you.

- Keep the circle
- Make a spiral
- Break the cycle

- Your decision is now your choice. Remember you don't have to change everything in one go. Sometimes it's easier to make a spiral.

- Stop thinking about how things happened in the past. Break the loop. This is a new day and a new you. Anything is possible if you believe it is.

- What would you do if you weren't afraid to try?

- Leave the comfort of your mind swindle and do things differently from now on.

- You can behave any way you choose.

- If you believe that you do not have a choice about how you respond, this is your mind swindle. Another you with another past and another belief system would behave another way.

- Stop worrying about what might happen and face problems only if they arise -not with FEAR but NOW!

- Notice the little victories where you are making small changes to behaviour patterns. Congratulate yourself. You are changing your conditioning. This will create positive reinforcers and remind you to behave a different way.

Food for thought before you move on:

Stop! Think! Become aware! What do you want to do?

Now you have the power to change, how will you change your life?

Remind yourself of what you want to change.

'I want to be ...'

It's time!

Part Seven

Change

So there you have it. Three choices: Keep the cycle; break the cycle; make a spiral. Altering this cycle in any way will alter behaviour patterns, belief systems and biological responses. If you continue to reinforce this new behaviour, you will continue to behave this new way. You will build new positive triggers to encourage this behaviour. Things will change.

It is up to the individuals to choose for themselves the way that is right for them. It is *your* responsibility to choose how you behave; it is *you* that it will ultimately affect. By now you will have come to realise that up until this point, your behaviour patterns and thought processes have been largely unconscious. In order to change, one must *consciously* change.

Change requires willpower and a desire for things to be different in some way. Up until this moment, you have been pre-programmed to behave a certain way. It is a case of quite literally reprogramming yourself to respond differently than you have done before. It can be done. It takes awareness and conscious effort. For many, it seems like hard work and they give up trying, and in the end nothing changes and they remain unhappy with parts of their life. If you believe that you can't change, things won't change; but by now you can hopefully see this is just your mind swindle playing tricks on you.

Beliefs

Beliefs are what make you. They are created by what you think and what you feel about yourself and the world around you. Up until now you have been taught what to believe by the people around you: family, peer groups, teachers, people that we meet etc. Anyone can have a strong influence upon what you believe by their words and actions. As you grow up, your mind is trying to make sense of the world and is making connections all the time. However, sometimes those connections are wrong.

Beliefs ultimately determine how you behave and are often nothing more than self-fulfilling prophesies. For example if you believe you are odd; you will behave oddly around other people and people will therefore find you odd. Your behaviour may make people steer clear of you. So far, how you have chosen to act is how you always have. It ties in with what you believe is the right thing to do.

Exercise:
What is the belief that holds you back?

Who taught you that?

Why did they teach you that? What did they gain?

Are your beliefs correct?

Are they part of your mind swindle?

Are you the person that you once believed you were?

How do you feel about that?

If you still feel bad look at what the belief is behind that. Is it true? You can eliminate the trigger. We did it way back in chapter 3 but the exercise is also in the appendix

If you feel ok, great, move on.

If this is **_not_** true, what *is*?

How do you feel about that?

How can you move on from here?

What can you alter to start to see a change?

Question your beliefs

Look at the chart on the next page. Start with '**You NOW**' on the top line and work your way down and around.

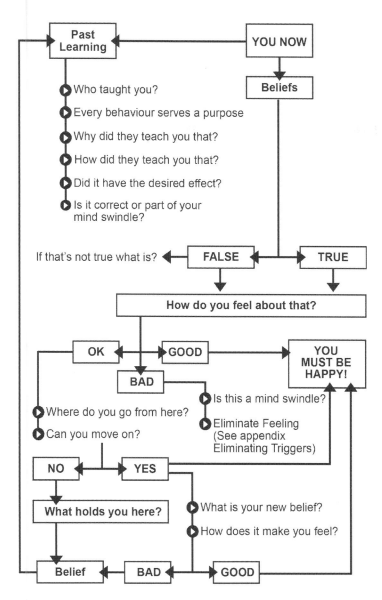

Figure 8: Questioning your beliefs

Thoughts create

The thoughts you have had in the past either consciously or subconsciously dictated how you have behaved. You have spent your entire life up until this point thinking about things a certain way.

What if these thoughts were wrong?

What if changing your thoughts helped to change your behaviour?

Simply changing from *'I can't'* to *'I am learning to'* can change the way you view things.

Exercise:
Become conscious of your unconscious thoughts.

What thoughts drive you?

How do they make you feel?

Are they correct?

How are you going to change your thought patterns?

What have you learned from reading this book?

Take time to think about it.

What thoughts are going to run your

---

unconscious now?

Now that you are changing, what do you have to keep reminding yourself about?

Let your new thought patterns make new connections in your brain.

Stay aware! Every time you feel bad, check if this is part of your mind swindle. Are you in a past/future loop?

Biology

The thoughts that you have can put you in a certain mood. This happens because of the chemicals running round your body. A different thought pattern will produce different chemicals and therefore produce different moods.

Because your mind swindle is so entrenched, you are predisposed to feel a certain way. Your body is used to making certain chemicals and your cells are used to picking up those chemicals. In order to feel differently on a continuous basis you have to make different chemicals, and this comes from a change in thought patterns and behaviour patterns. But even then, your body can slip back into old ways.

If you suffer with anxiety, remember adrenaline is addictive and when you are addicted there is no cut-off switch. It just keeps building. Like any addiction, it is difficult to give up. Thought processes create adrenaline. The part of your brain in charge of producing adrenaline (the hypothalamus) is also in charge of the body's balance of chemicals. You may find yourself with thoughts or behaviours that create adrenaline. You may even just get adrenaline rushes without any obvious reason as the hypothalamus instructs the body that you need more adrenaline to keep levels the same.[13]

Reminding yourself of this is helpful. Realising why you have these thoughts can help you control them. Bringing the unconscious into the conscious makes you aware about why you feel adrenalised. It gives you the control to stop it.

Exercise:
Have you been cooling your adrenaline?

If you feel adrenalised, STOP! Take a cooling breath. (See appendix)

Your thoughts create the chemicals that drive your body. Changing your thoughts will change your chemicals and change your feelings.

Have you noticed any change in mood yet?

---

[13] Open University Understanding depression and anxiety Open learn 2016

What moods would *you* like to be your dominant moods?

What mood do you feel right now?

Beliefs create behaviour

If you believe you can't do something, you won't. Learning that it is only your mind swindle that is stopping you, opens up new possibilities. Learning to look at your own limiting beliefs and challenging them enables you to see them for what they are - part of your mind swindle.

Exercise:
Imagine a situation where you wished that you behaved in a different way.

How would a different *you* with a different past and a different set of beliefs respond?

What is to stop you from behaving this way?

What do you imagine will happen?

Is this real?

Is it **F**alse **E**vidence **A**cting **R**eal?

Is it a past/future loop?

Is it your mind swindle playing tricks on you?

Would it happen for a different *you*?

You can stop the swindle if you choose too. It just takes conscious effort. The choice is yours.

Changing your beliefs will allow you to act a different way.

Now that you believe something different, how will you behave?

What will you do differently?

If you feel stuck, look back at the beliefs section on the previous pages.

Eliminate bad feelings the same as you eliminate triggers (See appendix)

Every behaviour serves a purpose

Everything we do has a reason. We believe (either consciously or subconsciously) that it serves a purpose. Up until now, much of your behaviour has been unconscious. Before, you behaved a certain way. What did you hope this behaviour would do for you? Why did you choose to act this way? Was it the best course of action to get the desired results? By starting to reflect we begin to make more of our behaviours conscious and therefore easier to change.

Exercise:

Think of a response you would like to change.

You respond that way because you have learned to.

What is the trigger?

What do you think your response does?

Are you correct?

What does it *actually* do?

If you have learned it, you can *unlearn* it.

Become aware. It's time to change!

We did an exercise for eliminating triggers in chapter 3. You can also find it in the appendix.

Differing realities

Everyone sees the world from their own perspective. They are looking at the world from their own reality. What they have grown up to believe about situations. How to think, feel and behave is a product of their mind swindle.

How one person sees things will be different to another person. Remember this when discussing things. Another person may misunderstand what you are trying to communicate. They are seeing things from their own perspective -their history, their beliefs, their biology, their mind swindle. Take time to listen before you speak. Communication is a two-way street.

Exercise:

How do you see someone else's behaviour?

How do they see it?

How do they see yours? (To them *you* are the situation.)

How does their behaviour serve their purpose?

What does it do for you?

What does your behaviour do for them?

What does your behaviour do for *you*?

If you continue to behave in a way that makes you unhappy in order to serve someone else's purpose, you will always remain unhappy. And they won't change unless it serves *their* purpose.

What is best for you?

You can choose what to do.

The Mind Swindle

Up until this point you have been programmed to think a certain way, feel a certain way and behave a certain way. Because of your past, you had very little choice. Behaviour patterns, triggers, thoughts and the world in which you lived determined what you did and how you did it.

You weren't aware that you had another choice.

Your mind swindle controlled everything.

Now you can see the past that you came from and decide if what you learned was correct.

You learned in one context and linked it to other aspects of your life.

Just because you learned it, doesn't mean it was correct.

Did it serve someone else's purpose for you to learn it?

Re-learning takes conscious effort. How many years have you been running these broken programs? The effort is worth it, if you become free to make your own choices: the choices that serve you best.

Working through your mind swindle

Take a look at the chart below. It is designed to show the mind swindle in it's simplest form. There is a large version in the appendix P242.

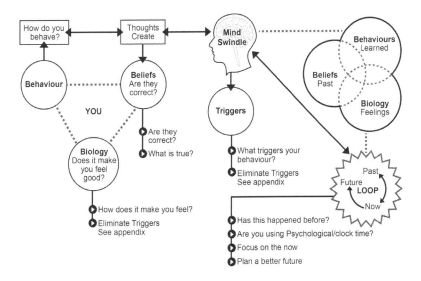

Figure 9. Working through your mind swindle

Final Activity – This is a lengthy activity, as you need to get to the core of what drives you to behave as you do. So take time to really think in this activity. Allow plenty of time to work through it. Some of the questions are repeated but bear with it – answer the questions as they arise. You can repeat this activity as many times as you like – for any behaviour that you *don't* like.

If you are stuck in a cycle of behaving a certain way, take a look at why and write it down. Take your time to think about and answer the following questions:

What is the belief that makes you behave like this?

Why do you think you should continue like this?

Now ask yourself if this is true?

Is your mind swindle playing tricks on you?

How do you feel about that?

If you have any uncomfortable feelings, look at where you can feel them in your body and eliminate them by just watching them until they disappear. (See appendix Eliminating triggers)

How would you like to behave instead?

If you stop the old behaviour and behave the way that you want to, what do you believe will happen?

Is this true or just a trick played by your mind swindle? A past/future loop maybe?

How do you feel about this?

Other than dictating how we behave now, does the past have any other use?

Does it have a life of its own?

Can you revisit it or change it?

Is it going to help you now?

What did the past teach you that held you to this behaviour for so long?

Again, is this true or just your mind swindle playing tricks on you?

How do you feel?

Again, if you have any uncomfortable feelings, look at where you feel them in your body and eliminate them by just watching them until they disappear. (See appendix Eliminating triggers)

Is there a different perspective that another person might see?

If you were another 'you' with another history and a different set of beliefs would you still be feeling the same?

How does this make you feel?

Could there be another way to act?

When you become aware, you can choose whether your way is still the right way. Will you let FEAR stop you from changing how to behave?

Again, if you have any uncomfortable feelings, look at where you can feel them in your body and eliminate them by just watching them until they disappear. (See appendix Eliminating triggers)

Do you want to change your programming now?

Behaviour patterns come from past experiences. You have been taught unconsciously that when 'X' happens, you feel 'Y' and do 'Z'. At the moment, you are preprogrammed to feel and behave a certain way. Biologically, your body becomes used to feeling a certain way.

How you think and what you believe produces the chemicals that make you feel and behave the way that you do. Your behaviour will reinforce the chemicals and continue to produce them. The cycle will continue until you consciously choose to change it.

Learning to be different doesn't happen overnight. Pay attention to the moods you find yourself in.

What are your dominant moods?

What are the emotions that drive you?

What emotions would you rather have?

Can you imagine them?

When would they be helpful?

Where and how would you use them?

What is stopping you at the moment is an unconscious belief that has its roots somewhere in the past. You are responding to unconscious triggers that make you feel and behave a certain way. Becoming conscious of this is the first step.

What is the belief stopping you?

Question it. Is it true?

Pay attention to those triggers. Once you start to become conscious of your triggers, you can choose whether to respond to them.

What is driving the trigger?

Where do they come from?

How do you feel just before your responses are triggered? Recognise that feeling. Give it a name. Do something different when you feel that feeling. The cooling breath perhaps.

Are the triggers still needed?

What would happen if you removed those triggers and started behaving differently?

Would everyone behave like you do or just someone

with your past and your belief system? Is it a broken program? Your Mind Swindle?

How do you feel just before the behaviour is triggered? Give it a name (e.g. hurt, irritated etc.)
Where can you feel in your body?
Again, eliminate the trigger. (See appendix)

The aim is not knowing what you *don't* want but knowing what you *do* want.

Remember you are here *now*. The past has gone and has taught you things and these are not necessarily true. Based on your past you predict the future. Thoughts of this imagined future create an emotion; an emotion that you have now. This is your problem *now*.

What is your emotion? How does it make you feel?

Is it true or a trick of your mind swindle?

When you recognise the emotions, you can eliminate them by using the same method as eliminating triggers (see appendix)

If you are finding it difficult to change things, it's because you are stuck somewhere in your mind swindle, a past/future loop, a belief or a behaviour pattern that you have not explored yet.

Become aware of what it is.

What is holding you to that behaviour?

Restart this final activity (or even the final chapter if it's helpful) with *this* as the problem that is making you feel stuck in this cycle of behaviour. You have to get to the root of what is stopping you from change. You have to keep going round the activity until you see how to make the change and are ready to try.

Is your problem true or a trick of your mind swindle?

Do you want it to continue?

Can you use clock time to change things and plan for a different future? Stop the cycle. There are always choices if you dare to look.

Question your beliefs and decide how best to make your change.

Look at **Part 5 Things that may stop you**.

Learn from past mistakes. If you want to be different then _be_ *different. Just because you used to act a certain way, it doesn't mean that you can't begin to behave differently. It takes a conscious choice. Don't say 'I can't help it', 'I am not confident enough' or 'I am grieving'. Saying 'I can't do it' means you won't be able to do it. If you start looking at what you* _can_ *change and put it into practice, things* _will_ *start to change.*

It is up to you to make the changes that are right for you. No one else will.

Your life. Your choices. Your responsibility.

Remember to go back and repeat this final activity as many times as you need to make the changes that you want.

Take a look at the chart on the next page. It is designed to show you how to work through your mind swindles. You should now have all the tools in your toolbox but the appendix will help you.

Start with Beliefs and work your way round.

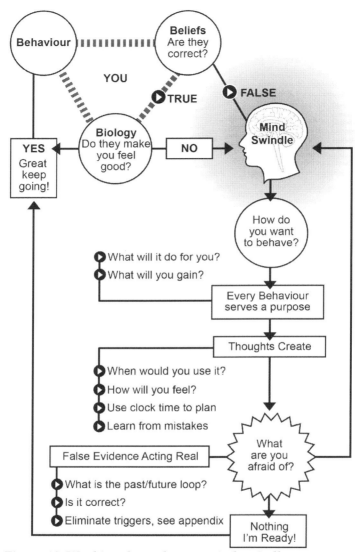

Figure 10: Working through your mind swindle.

So how do you change your mind swindles once you see them? Simple answer: you start to change them.

Recognising them for what they are and being prepared to do something about them.

It isn't always easy to change who you are. You will certainly encounter challenges along the way. Who *you* are today is the product of *everything* you have encountered and *all* that you have learned up to this point. It is about leaving the past in the past. Let it go. It may take time to re-learn beliefs and behaviours but you *can* do it. It is part of your growth. You have spent years learning to be you. Now you have to consciously learn another way.

Things will turn around and you will notice a change. When you throw a pebble into the pond, the effects ripple out. It takes time. Just staying focused on what you can do now will keep you on the right track.

Remember the only thing at this point that has changed is you. You have learned that the beliefs you once thought of as true were not correct. You have recognised that you have been running broken programs -products of your mind swindle. You have learned that you do not have to behave as you always have and that you are free to choose to behave a different way.

It is at this point you have made the decision to change and your behaviour is going to alter.

Now you will start interacting with others as the new and improved you. Where you usually behaved one way, you will start to behave differently.

People around you will notice the new *you*. If your problem lies with another person, the new *you* will soon become apparent. They will respond to you differently. They will *have* to. Some people may like the change; others may not. Remember people work for a positive intention but only from their point of view. It might suit them better for you to behave the old way. They may try and change you back by responding as they always have or even stronger to try to get a reaction. Take a cooling breath and stop yourself from responding. Keep reinforcing the new behaviour with them as well as you. It is a learning curve for everyone!

Remember that you can't change other people, only yourself. They will react differently because you are different. If you continue to act differently, they will learn that this is the new you and decide for themselves how best to deal with it. They will settle into a new behaviour. Whether this is positive or negative depends on the circumstances.

You can't second-guess their behaviour towards

you – that is your mind swindle creating a past/future loop. You will just have to wait and see what will be. They might surprise you! Now you must decide if their new behaviour is right for you. You still have the choices: keep the cycle; make a spiral; break the cycle.

Only you can decide what is right for you, and if you stop running broken programs from past behaviour or living in fear of the future, you can decide what is best for you *now*. This is how we make the change.

Remember, most of our behaviour patterns are unconscious. You are allowed to make mistakes. When you become conscious of an old pattern, *STOP*. Use the cooling breath (See appendix). You can change it back again. Learn to do what is right for you, and as you get accustomed to doing so; it gets easier to change back again to your new patterns. It is simply learning to act differently. You have to become conscious of what you must do.

Only you are responsible for the way you act and only you can decide the best way for you to behave. The best way of doing this is to stop and view your choices. Look at what holds you back. Free yourself of past/future loops and automatic responses.

Instead of living by what *could* happen, start dealing with what *is* happening. Life becomes so much simpler. Accept each day as it comes and remember that if you expect yourself to feel a certain way, then you *will*. You are in effect telling your body which chemicals to make.

You can create yourself anew and behave anyway you choose because without your mind swindle running unconscious programs in the background, you are free to behave how you feel is right now.

Eventually, living in the now will become as natural as living in your past/future loops like you used to. It will become an automatic response. You will become happier and more content with life. I am not saying that life will be perfect. You will still face life's challenges, but living in the now gives you a chance to deal with things more positively. You can stop responding automatically and give yourself more conscious choices.

Only *you* can change you. Sitting and complaining about what's wrong and not doing anything about it is crazy. We are however, all guilty of this sometimes. Until we decide to alter things, how do we expect things to change?

Remember that guilt will stop you from changing so you need to release yourself from it (see part five). What you have done before doesn't matter as long as you have learned from your mistakes. Learn your lesson and move on.

People work for their own advantage and their behaviour serves a purpose. Every behaviour pattern you have will have served some purpose for you on some level at some time, or so you believed. It's time to look at the pattern and decide if you want to keep it. Is it still helpful to you?

Without the constraints of your old behaviour patterns, you are free to act a different way. Choose the best way for you to behave now.

Learn to see things another way. You can begin to believe what you want. What you believe comes from what you have learned and you have been learning something new in this book.

Beliefs are a product of your past. Just because you believed it to be true, it doesn't mean it was true. It is only past learning. You learned it because of the time and place you were in back then. You *can* be mistaken. You *can* learn something else.

Beliefs *do* change. It is a natural part of growth.

To be truly happy we must stop and look at why we aren't. This is usually the hardest step. It is your mind swindle playing tricks on you. It is only then that you can start to change things. Becoming the person you want to be brings you happiness. Your happiness is your responsibility. How you live your life is up to you.

The choices are yours but first you must become aware that you have choices. I hope after reading this far, you see that you do.

Conclusion

- Can you see your mind swindle for what it is now?

- Up until now, you have been an unconscious slave to the chemicals that are being made by your mind and body.

- You respond without question to your thoughts.

- You are spurred into action by triggers and behaviour patterns that have been made sometime in the past.

- Do these still serve you best?

- Many people will have started this book at their lowest point. *'I do not want this!'*

- Well what *do* you want? You have to know what you want to become. Otherwise, how will your mind and body know how to act?

- How *would* it be if it were <u>not</u> like this? How would you behave? How would you feel? Take time to consider this.

- The changes will ripple out to other areas of your life. How would life alter?

- Question your beliefs. Are they correct?

- If you could wipe away your past conditioning... If you believed something different... How might this be?

- How would a different *you* with a different history be thinking, feeling and behaving now?

- If you stopped worrying about what might happen and just did what you felt was right, how might you act now?

- Now you have taken time to consider this, change is only a step away.

- The key is to become conscious of your behaviour patterns and decide if this is still your best course of action. It is about learning to respond differently.

- You alone are responsible for *you* and your behaviour.

- It is up to you to teach others that *you* have changed.

- The only thing that will stop *you* is your mind swindle.

- Use your tools (see appendix) to free yourself of your mind swindle

- Start the change NOW!

Things to consider:

Is now a good time to move on and do something different?

Things will not change unless you do.

Start becoming the new *you*.

Start changing *NOW!*

Appendix

The Cooling Breath

Learn to calm your anxiety

Take a deep breath in through your nose

Make a circle with your lips and blow the breath out!

- Put your hand on your belly
- Breathe in through your nose! Take notice of your hand on your belly rising. Keep practising until you can do it
- Blow your breath out through your mouth!
- Pause if you want
- Breathe in! Imagine the air coming in through your nose and filling your belly with air
- Breathe out!
- Relax
- After each breath there is a pause.
- Breathe in through your nose. Take a big belly full of air
- Make a circle with your lips and blow the air out
- Relax
- Breathe in through your nose and take a big belly full of air

- Put your hand up to your face and blow your breath out onto your hand
- Allow the pause. Take your time!
- Take a deep breath in and move your hand away from your face a little
- Make a circle with your lips
- Breathe out
- Relax as you feel your breath against your skin
- Allow the pause
- Breathe deeply through your nose and out through your lips
- Move your hand a little away from your face.
- Continue the exercise and each time you blow out keep moving your hand further away until you can no longer feel your breath against your skin or until you are calm
- You can now think straight

Once you have mastered this you'll be able to breathe in through your nose and blow your breath out through your mouth and use the cooling breath any time and any place, and you'll immediately start to feel the benefits.

Make yourself calm

Learn to relax more

Think clearer

Eliminating Triggers

An Exercise in Eliminating Past Triggers

Triggers always cause you to act a certain way. Your response is both automatic and unconscious. Something triggers that response. You learned it in the past. You are reminded to act that way by something or somebody else.

The answer is to eliminate the trigger.

Before you respond to the trigger you will feel something, somewhere in the body. It is usually unconscious so you have to bring it to the conscious. Give it a name. So *'Just before I react I feel X'*.

Rather than respond as you always have, stop. Look at it.

What causes it?

What is the driving emotion?

Where do you feel it?

Now at this point people get uncomfortable. They do not like the feeling it produces. They would rather not look at it. The mind starts to chatter with reasons or excuses. It is at this point most people look away and continue to use the trigger.

You need to act as an outsider looking in and just watch it. It may have rhyme and reason but it doesn't need any commentary from your mind.

Stop and look at the feeling it evokes. It doesn't need to be analysed as right or wrong. It is simply an old behaviour pattern. You just have to watch the emotion and see how it changes. Ride the emotion and allow it to run its course, keeping yourself fully focused on it. Ignore the desire to respond or to think about it. The emotion is like a wave rising before it falls. When it goes away, it has played itself out. Your neurons have learned to fire differently. You dissolve the need to behave a certain way.

Just go back and look at what drives it again. Does it feel the same? Are there still negative feelings? Maybe in a different part of the body. If there is, eliminate the trigger again until there isn't a negative feeling.

You are free of that trigger. You are free to act a different way. How will you act next time the same thing happens? You have to make a plan of action. You are now free to choose.

Because we have been behaving a certain way for some time there is probably more than one trigger. We have learned behaviour patterns over and over again. We respond similarly to different stimuli so triggers can, and do stack up.

———

You may need to look at the same emotional triggers more than once for different stimuli. They may sit in different places within the body.

The trick is to become aware of what they are - an automatic response to a given situation.

Once you start recognizing the feeling that comes just before you react, you can start changing the response before you feel compelled to act. Take a cooling breath and change the response.

We can eliminate them and learn to act a different way. You just have to start thinking about HOW you want to act now?

The Past/Future Loop

The past/future loop is when you second-guess the future from what has happened in the past. You respond in the moment as though what you believe might happen were true, without question to whether it is. This usually brings about a similar outcome.

If you could let go of the past and learn from it, you could choose to behave a different way, creating a whole different response and a whole different future.

Focus on the now.

If a different *you* with a different past would be acting differently then so can you. If you weren't stuck responding the same way as you have before, what could you do now?

What do you need to be doing? Is there anything that you need to learn?

Take a deep breath!

Decide what you need to be doing to achieve a better outcome for you.

You can't change other people, only yourself

What are you going to do now?

Now you know that you have choice, you can decide.

If you get any uncomfortable feelings, you are in a past/future loop. You can eliminate the feelings by becoming aware that this is what's happening.

Eliminate feelings the same way as you do for triggers. (See the last appendix)

Take a deep breath and do it.

NOW

Such a simple concept and yet often overlooked by most people.

NOW: This moment that you are living in. Not thinking about the past. Not thinking about what might happen in the future. NOW. This moment. What is happening with you?

TAKE A BREATH!
A deep COOLING breath.

At this moment, how are you feeling?
Are you stressed about the future?
Are you upset about the past?
Are you happy and full of joy?
How would you like to be?

If you are upset about the past, you can't focus on what is happening around you now.

If you are anxious about the future, you might be rash and make mistakes.

STOP AND TAKE A BREATH!

Fill your belly with air. In through your nose and blow out through your lips. Exhale!

PAUSE. Repeat.

———

Who Do You Want To Be?

Once you are free from your past you can change anything.

You can train yourself to be a different you.

If you don't have to be the same old *you* anymore, you can be a new and different *you*.

How do you want to behave?

Do you want to be the complete opposite or just make small *changes*?

How will you walk and talk?

How will you behave?

How will it change you?

How will you feel?

Who do *you* want to be?

Three Choices

Now that you know where you are and you know where you want to be. The difference between these is your problem. Once you know where your problem lies, you have three choices

Accept the problem

Stop the problem

Change the problem

Choose

Before you read this book, the workings of your mind and body were unconscious. A machine; wired to respond in a certain way to a set of triggers it had made for itself. It made certain chemicals that dictated what and how you would feel.

Even when you stopped to think about what you should do, you didn't choose from all of the many possibilities. Most possibilities were shut off to you. Ignored by your subconscious as irrelevant or something you wouldn't be able to do.

NOW YOU CAN CHOOSE

Question your beliefs

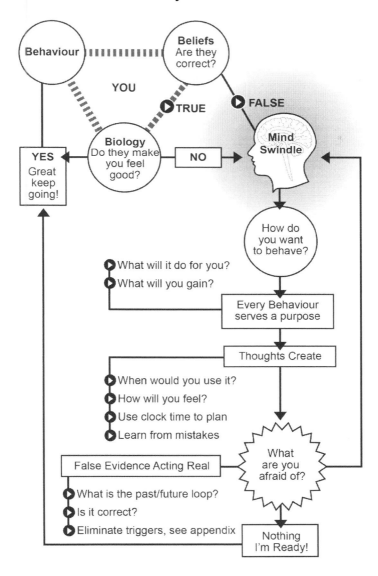

Breaking down your mind swindle

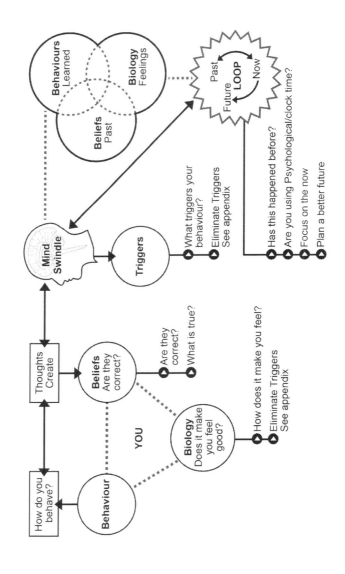

Working through your mind swindle

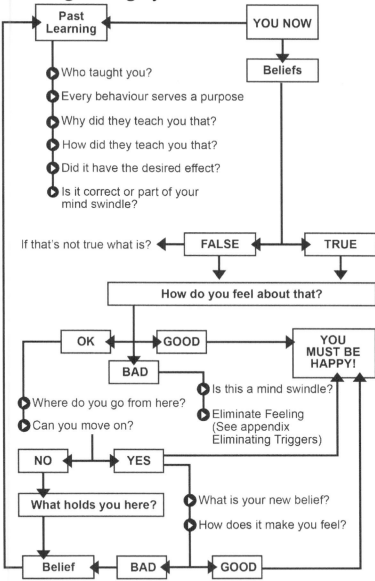

Bibliography

Davey Basiro, Halliday Tim and Hirst Mark: *Human Biology and Health: An Evolutionary Approach.* The Open University *(2001)*

Davey Basiro, Gray Alistair, Seale Clive: *Health and Disease: A reader.* The Open University (2001)

Bandler and Grinder: *Using Your Brain for a Change.* Real Peoples Press (1985)

Grinder John: *Transformations.* Real Peoples Press (1981)

Heller Joseph: *Catch-22.* Vintage (1994)

Heller Steven: *Monsters and Magical Sticks.* Original Falcon Press (1987)

Jones Gary, Jones Geoff: *Human Biology for A2.* Cambridge University Press (2005)

Krishnamurti: *Freedom from the Known.* HarperSanFrancisco (1969)

Lipton Bruce H Ph.D: *The Biology of Belief.* Hay House (2005)

O'Connor Joseph: *Ways of NLP.* Element (2001)

O'Connor Joseph, Lages Andrea: *Coaching with NLP.* Element (2004)

Open Learn: *Cell Signalling.* Open University (2016)

Open Learn: Emotions and Emotional Disorders. Open University (2015)

Open Learn: *Understanding Depression and Anxiety.* Open University *(2015)*

Pert Candice PhD *Molecules of Emotion.* Simon & Schuster: (1997)

Simpkins J, Williams J. I: *Advanced Human Biology.* CollinsEducational (1993)

Tolle Eckhart: *The Power of Now.* Hodder and Stoughton (2001)

Tolle Eckhart: *Practicing the Power of Now.* Hodder and Stoughton (2002)

Tolle Eckhart: *A NEW EARTH.* Hodder and Stoughton (2005)

Printed in Great Britain
by Amazon